Alexander P. Saccaro

TRAINING
Englische Grammatik
5./6. Schuljahr

Beilage: Lösungsheft

Ernst Klett Verlag für Wissen und Bildung
Stuttgart · Dresden

 Gedruckt auf Papier, das aus chlorfrei gebleichtem
Zellstoff hergestellt wurde.

Die Deutsche Bibliothek – CIP-Einheitsaufnahme

Saccaro, Alexander Peter:
Training englische Grammatik:
5./6. Schuljahr / Alexander P. Saccaro. –
1. Aufl. – Stuttgart; Dresden:
Klett-Verl. für Wissen und Bildung, 1995
ISBN 3-12-922116-6

© Ernst Klett Verlag für Wissen und Bildung GmbH, Stuttgart 1995
Satz: Service-Center, Schwabenverlag AG, Ostfildern
Druck: Wilhelm Röck, Weinsberg
Illustrationen: Andreas Florian, Lübeck
Einbandgestaltung: Hitz und Mahn, Stuttgart
ISBN 3-12-922116-6

Inhalt

Einleitung

Was soll dieses Trainingsbuch?

Es ist eine alte Tatsache: Wer lernt, macht Fehler. Doch sollte man bestimmte Fehler nicht immer wieder machen, zumal sie sich leicht vermeiden lassen, wenn man etwas aufpaßt. Dazu möchte dieses Trainingsbuch beitragen: Es soll dir helfen, typische Fehler zu vermeiden.

Was du dazu tun mußt

Dazu mußt du allerdings auch selbst etwas tun, denn ganz ohne Lernen geht die Sache nicht. Wenn du nicht bereit bist, z. B. die Formen von *to be* so zu lernen, daß du sie auch im Schlaf aufsagen kannst, wird dir auch ein noch so großes Verständnis für die englische Grammatik nur wenig nutzen. Denn Sprachen sind keine Mathematik. Dort gibt es viel zu verstehen, aber wenig zu lernen; bei den Sprachen dagegen gibt es wenig zu verstehen, aber viel (auswendig) zu lernen.

Wie dieses Trainingsbuch aufgebaut ist

Dieses Trainingsbuch umfaßt den wesentlichen Stoff der ersten beiden Lernjahre Englisch. Es ist in 19 Kapitel eingeteilt, die du unabhängig von einander durchnehmen kannst. Die Anordnung der einzelnen Kapitel lehnt sich an die Durchnahme des Grammatikstoffes in der Schule an, so daß du dieses Buch schon früh benutzen kannst – zum Teil sogar parallel zum Unterricht. Die Übungen sind nach ihrem Schwierigkeitsgrad angeordnet und auf typische Fehler abgestimmt.

Wie du dieses Buch benutzen solltest

Du kannst das Buch Kapitel für Kapitel durcharbeiten und so deine Grammatikkenntnisse rundherum auffrischen. Du kannst aber auch gezielt nur den Stoff einzelner Kapitel üben – als Vorbereitung auf eine Klassenarbeit zum Beispiel oder um einzelne Lücken zu schließen. Das Ergebnis deiner Anstrengungen kannst du danach – bitte nicht vorher! – mit den Lösungen im Lösungsheft vergleichen.

Richtiges Lernen

Zum Schluß noch ein Wort zum Lernen selbst. Wie du vielleicht schon gemerkt hast, sind gute Schülerinnen und Schüler oft nicht deshalb gut, weil sie sehr viel lernen, sondern weil sie regelmäßig lernen. Schlechte Schülerinnen und Schüler sind dagegen oft solche, die meist sehr viel in ganz wenig Zeit zu lernen versuchen und als Folge sehr viel in ganz kurzer Zeit wieder vergessen. Versuch also nicht, dies Büchlein in einem Rutsch durchzumachen, sondern verteile dein Lernen und arbeite regelmäßig. Was bleibt, ist dir bei der Arbeit mit diesem Buch Spaß und Erfolg zu wünschen; denn fehlt das eine, bleibt das andere oft aus.

Nouns

Substantive

Weißt du noch, was Substantive bzw. Nomen sind? Grob gesagt, sind es Wörter, mit denen wir Personen, Tiere, Sachen, Gegenstände und abstrakte Begriffe wie Eigenschaften und Gefühle bezeichnen. Viele dieser Substantive können auch im Plural gebraucht werden.

Die regelmäßige Bildung des Plurals

Im allgemeinen bildet man den Plural im Englischen, indem man an die Singularform ein **-s** (nach Zischlauten ein **-es**, wenn kein **-e** vorhanden ist) anhängt:

Singular	Plural		Singular	Plural
a farm	farm**s**		a bus	bus**es**
a hen	hen**s**		a sponge	spong**es**

– auslautendes **-y** wird nach Konsonant zu **-ies**: a bab**y**   bab**ies**
– auslautendes **-fe** wird meist zu **-ves**:   a kni**fe**   kni**ves**

Unregelmäßige Pluralformen

a man	two m**e**n		a f**oo**t	two f**ee**t
a wom**a**n	three wom**e**n		a g**oo**se	ten g**ee**se
a child	five child**ren**		a m**ou**se	three m**i**c**e**

Training 1: Mr Mason's farm

Mr Mason is Tom's grandad. He has got a farm near York. Look at the picture of his farm.

a) *What people and animals are there on the farm?*
b) *Make a list of all the nouns. Put the singular nouns in the plural and the plural nouns in the singular.*

Example:	a farmhouse	farmhouses
	a wife	_____

Training 2: Animals, animals

There are other animals on a farm, too.

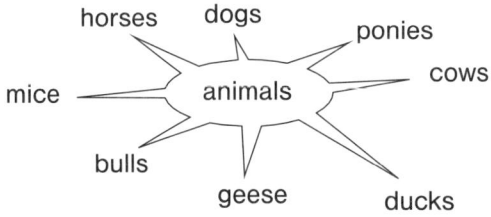

What is the singular of these nouns?

Training 3: Mr Mason's birthday

Fill in the right nouns.

There are a lot of _____, _____

and _____ on Mr Mason's farm today. They have all got

_____ for Mr Mason because it is his birthday. Look at

those two _____ over there; the big boy is Tom and the

small boy is Timmy. They have got presents, too. Tom's present is a book about

farm animals. Timmy has got something in his _____, too.

But it is not a _____, it is only his old

_____. Poor teddy! One _____ is missing and

one _____, too, and it is half-blind because one

_____ is gone. Timmy has got a present for his grandad, too.

It is a wonderful picture of three big _____. They are in

the kitchen and they are eating grandpa's birthday _____.

Look at that man over there! That's Tom's grandad, Mr Mason. He is a farmer, but today he is not wearing his old trousers, his old shirt and his old shoes. He has got his best clothes on because it is his birthday. Mrs Mason is wearing her best clothes, too. She is not wearing her old jeans, but a nice blouse, a new skirt and some nice tights.

clothes, jeans, trousers und *tights* (= Strumpfhosen) werden im Englischen immer im Plural gebraucht.
Der unbestimmte Artikel *a/an* ist vor diesen Substantiven nicht möglich.

Training 4: Kate's clothes

Look at this girl. It's Kate, Tom's sister. Well, it's grandpa's birthday, but she has got all her old clothes on.

Complete the sentences.

PULLOVER

BLOUSE

JEANS

TIGHTS

Look at her old pullover.

   It is dirty.

Look at her old tights.

   There _____ holes

   in _____ .

Look at her old jeans.

   _____ too small.

Look at her old blouse.

   _____ not clean.

Her clothes _____ really awful!

Training 5: Your clothes

a) *What are you wearing now?*

b) *What clothes do you like best?*

Auch *police* und *people* (= Leute) werden im Englischen immer wie Plural-wörter gebraucht.
Homework steht dagegen im Englischen immer im Singular.

Help! Where **are** the police?
Some people give us **too much** homework!

The personal pronoun

Das Personalpronomen

Das Personalpronomen als Subjekt

Where is Kate?	**She**	is here.
Where is Tom?	**He**	is at school.
Where is your book?	**It**	isn't here.
	Subjekt	

Pronomen stehen immer für (= pro) ein Substantiv (= Nomen). Ist das Pronomen das Subjekt eines Satzes, so lauten seine Formen:

I	**you**	**he**	**she**	**it**	**we**	**you**	**they**
(ich)	(du/Sie)	(er)	(sie)	(es)	(wir)	(ihr/Sie)	(sie)
	Singular					Plural	

It steht für Sachen; *they* kann für Sachen und Personen stehen. Alle anderen Personalpronomen stehen für Personen.

Training 1: Where are they?

Answer these questions. Use pronouns in your answers.

1. Where is Mr Mason?

(on the farm)

(in the house)

2. Where is Mrs Mason?

3. Where is Tom?

(at school)

4. Where is Tom's bike?

(at school, too)

(on the floor)

(on his potty)

5. Where is Timmy?

6. Where are his toys?

7. Where are his clothes?

(on his bed)

8. Where is Kate?

(not at home)

(with her)

9. Where is her girlfriend?

10. Where are Kate and Jenny?

(in the park)

Training 2: At school

Teachers ask a lot of questions. Ask and answer them.

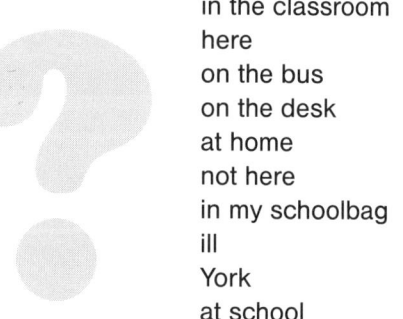

		in the classroom
	Tom and Mike?	here
	your homework?	on the bus
	your English book?	on the desk
Where is	your book?	at home
Where are	Christine?	not here
	the register?	in my schoolbag
	they from?	ill
	you from?	York
	Kate?	at school

Das Personalpronomen als Objekt

Personalpronomen können auch Objekt eines Satzes sein. Ihre Formen lauten dann:

		me	(mir/mich)
		you	(dir/dich/Ihnen)
Tom	can help	**him**	(ihm/ihn)
Kate	can see	**her**	(ihr/sie)
		it	(ihm/es)
		us	(uns)
		you	(euch/Ihnen)
		them	(ihnen/sie)
		Objekt	

Im Englischen macht man bei den Pronomen keinen Unterschied zwischen dem indirekten und direkten Objekt; die Formen sind gleich. Wie bei den Subjektpronomen steht *it* für eine Sache; *them* kann für Sachen und Personen stehen.

Die Objektform des Personalpronomens steht im Englischen auch nach Präpositionen:

Wait for **me**! Look at **her**!
Look at **him**! Wait for **them**!

Training 3: Looking for things and persons

Answer the questions. Use pronouns.

1. Where are my clothes?
2. Where is my book?
3. Where are you, Kate?
4. Where is Mike?
5. Where are Tom and Jenny?
6. Where are my photos?

7. Where are my keys?
8. Where is my money?
9. Where is Dad?
10. Where is your potty, Timmy?
11. Where is my teddy?
12. Where are my trousers?

I can't find _____ . I can't see _____ . I can't hear _____ .

Training 4: Asking Timmy

Fill in the missing pronouns.

Kate: Where are you, Timmy?

           I can't see _____ .

Timmy: _____ 'm here.

Kate: Where is your potty?

Timmy: _____ 's not here.

           I can't find _____ .

Kate: Where is your teddy?

Timmy: _____ 's in my bed. I can

           see _____ from here.

Kate: Where are your trousers?

           I can't see _____ .

Timmy: I really don't know.

Kate: Come on, Timmy, where are _____ ?

Timmy (crying):   _____ are in my room.

Kate: Why are _____ crying, Timmy?

Timmy (still crying): I don't like these trousers. _____ are bad trousers.

Kate: Why, Timmy? Are _____ wet again?

Timmy (still crying): Yes, _____ are.

Kate: Don't cry, Timmy. Let's wash _____ . Help _____ .

Training 5: Looking for Timmy's trousers

Kate is upstairs in Timmy's room. She is looking for his trousers, but she can't find them. Complete the sentences.

Kate: Timmy, where are _____? Help _____ to look for _____ .

Are _____ under your bed?

Timmy: No, _____ aren't. _____ aren't there.

Kate: Where are _____ then? Let _____ guess. Are _____ in

your bed?

Timmy: No, _____ aren't in my bed. _____ are in my teddy's bed.

Kate: In your teddy's bed? Where is _____?

Timmy: _____ 's here.

Kate: But why are _____ in your teddy's bed, Timmy?

Timmy: It's my teddy who makes _____ wet, not me.

Kate: Then call your teddy and tell _____ to help _____ .

The definite and the indefinite article

Kapitel 3

Der bestimmte und der unbestimmte Artikel

Der unbestimmte Artikel

a) Formen

a [ə]	**an** [ən]
a book	**an** apple
a yellow car	**an** empty car
a nice uncle	**an** uncle
a uniform	**an** old uniform

Der unbestimmte Artikel hat im Englischen zwei Formen: *a* und *an*. Vor einem folgenden Vokal steht *an*, vor einem folgenden Konsonant *a*. Vor dem Halbvokal [j] (wie in *unit, uniform, yellow*) steht *a*.

Training 1: Tom's schoolbag

Do you pack your schoolbag every day? Well, Tom doesn't. There are a lot of things in Tom's schoolbag:

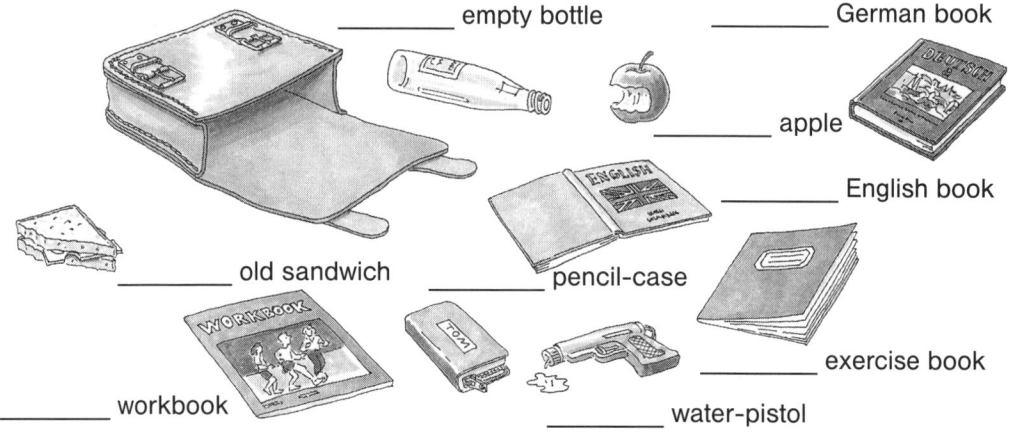

_____ empty bottle

_____ German book

_____ apple

_____ English book

_____ old sandwich

_____ pencil-case

_____ exercise book

_____ workbook

_____ water-pistol

b) Zum Gebrauch des unbestimmten Artikels

Tom has got **a** new girlfriend.
Her father is **a** taxi-driver.
She's ill today; she's got **a** headache and **a** temperature.

Der unbestimmte Artikel bezeichnet einzelne Dinge oder Personen. Im Unterschied zum Deutschen steht er bei Berufsbezeichnungen und bei bestimmten Ausdrücken wie *to have (got) a headache/a temperature* (= Kopfweh, Fieber haben).

Training 2: Who are they?

Example: 1. He is a milkman.

1. He brings the milk in the morning.

2. He brings you letters and parcels.

3. You go to him when you want to buy sausages.

4. He sells you all kind of vegetables.

5. She helps you to find what you want when you are in a shop.

6. She works for a newspaper.

7. He comes when your house is on fire.

8. He helps animals when they are ill.

Der bestimmte Artikel

a) Die Aussprache des bestimmten Artikels

the boy
the car
the uniform
the yellow book
[ðə]

the other girl
the English car
the old uniform
the easy unit
[ðɪ]

Wie du weißt, gibt es im Englischen nur eine Form des bestimmten Artikels. Seine Aussprache richtet sich nach dem folgenden Wort. Vor einem Vokal wird *the* [ðɪ], vor einem Konsonant und [j] wird er [ðə] ausgesprochen.

Training 3: What's right?

Say the words with the [ðə] *or* [ðɪ]. *Example:* [ðə] box, [ðɪ] empty box.

_____ old women   _____ young girls   _____ American cars

_____ English children   _____ silly answer   _____ difficult question

_____ example   _____ bad ideas   _____ school uniforms

_____ yellow apples   _____ afternoons   _____ empty pages

b) Zum Gebrauch des bestimmten Artikels

1. **The** colours of Tom's school uniform are blue and grey. **The** girls must wear a grey skirt and **the** boys must wear grey trousers.

1. Der bestimmte Artikel steht immer, wenn es sich um bestimmte Personen oder Sachen handelt.

2. **Not** all boys and girls in Britain like school uniforms.

2. Wenn diese nicht näher bestimmt sind, steht der bestimmte Artikel nicht.

3. Tom goes to school by bus. Some children go there by train.

3. Der bestimmte Artikel steht auch nicht bei Eigennamen im Singular und bei Verkehrsmitteln, wenn man sagen will, wie man irgendwo hinkommt.

Bei Wörtern wie *bed* und *school* steht kein Artikel, wenn man ausdrücken will, was man dort tut. Ist dagegen das Möbelstück oder das Gebäude gemeint, so steht der bestimmte Artikel:

Let's go **to bed**.
= Gehen wir ins Bett (= schlafen).

Let's look under **the bed**.
= Schauen wir unter dem Bett nach.

He goes **to school**.
= Er geht zur Schule (= in den Unterricht).

His mother is going **to the school**.
= Seine Mutter geht in die Schule.

Training 4: Definite article or not?

Complete the sentences.

1. _____ boys like _____ girls.

2. _____ Tom likes _____ Jenny.

3. Do you like _____ boys in your class?

4. Do you usually like _____ girls more than _____ boys?

5. What about _____ girls in your class? Are they nice?

6. Which of _____ boys/girls do you like best?

7. Who is _____ nicest boy/girl in your class?

8. What's _____ name of the girl/boy you like best?

9. Are _____ girls/boys in your class good at English?

10. Are _____ boys as clever as _____ girls? What do you think?

Training 5: Jenny

Definite article or not? Complete the sentences.

Jenny is not Tom's sister, she is _____ Tom's friend. She lives in_____ Apple

Street. _____ Apple Street is a small street in _____ north of _____ York. In win-

ter she goes to _____ school by _____ bus, in summer she goes to _____

school by _____ bike. _____ Tom is in her class. She doesn't like all _____ girls

and boys in her class, but she likes _____ Tom very much. She thinks he is

_____ nicest boy in her class. But Jenny doesn't only like _____ Tom, she also

likes _____ maths. _____ maths is _____ subject she likes best. Before _____

tests, she always helps _____ Tom. Jenny also likes _____ pets. She hasn't got a

pet yet, but she can have a pet for her birthday.

Training 6: Jenny is ill

Where is a definite or indefinite article missing?

Jenny goes to _____ same school as _____ Tom. Sometimes Tom's father takes

them to _____ school in _____ morning. _____ school they go to is _____ big

school. There are a lot of _____ pupils at Jenny's school, and not all of them like

_____ school. But Jenny does; she likes _____ school because most of _____

teachers she has got are really good. Today she can't go to _____ school; she

must stay in _____ bed, but she hasn't got _____ temperature. She's got _____

cold and _____ bad headache. She feels terrible and she doesn't want to eat

anything. She just wants to see _____ doctor and stay _____ bed. Poor Jenny!

Training 7: How can you get there?

Today there is a geography lesson. The children are talking about how they can get to other towns or countries. Be careful! Tom and the other children live in York.

<u>Example:</u> What about London? How can you get there?
     I can get there by train.

Germany

Scotland

Ireland

Denmark

France

The Isle of Wight

Wales

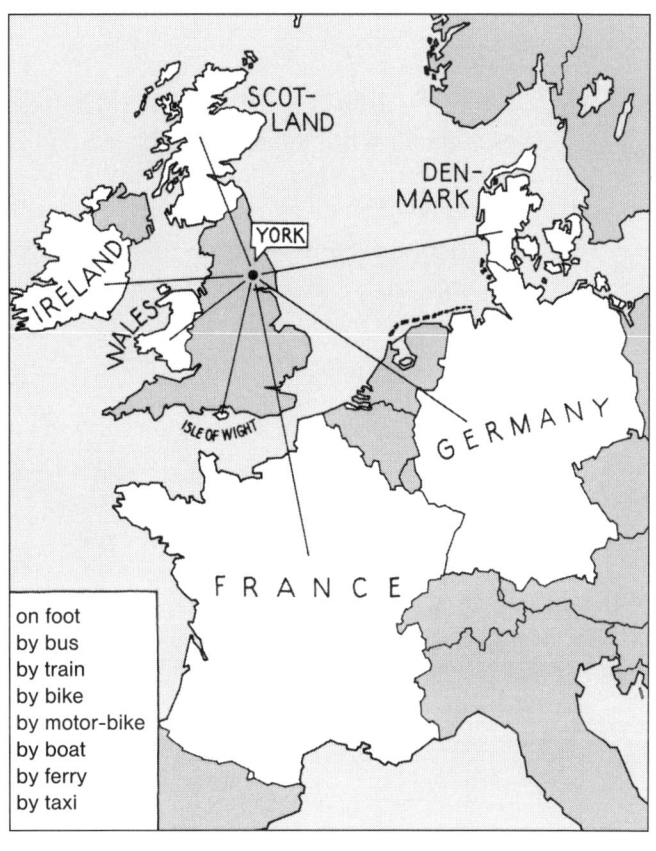

on foot
by bus
by train
by bike
by motor-bike
by boat
by ferry
by taxi

Nouns and their determiners

Kapitel 4

Substantive und ihre Begleiter

Englische wie deutsche Substantive stehen nicht immer allein. Sie werden häufig von anderen Wörtern „begleitet", die sie näher bestimmen. In der deutschen Grammatik nennt man diese Wörter daher „Begleiter"; in der englischen Grammatik heißen sie *determiners*. Zu diesen Begleitern gehören unter anderem:

Die Possessivbegleiter

Formen:

This isn't	**my**	book.
Is it	**your**	book?
No, it isn't. It's	**her**	book.
No, it's	**his**	book.
Oh, no. Is it	**your**	book, Tom and Kevin?
Let's see. No, it isn't	**our**	book. Perhaps it's the girls' book.
Yes, it is. It's	**their**	book.

My, your etc. drücken Besitz oder Zugehörigkeit aus. Mit Ausnahme von *their,* das sich auch auf Sachen beziehen kann, beziehen sich *my, your* usw. immer auf Personen. Dabei kann *your* verschiedene Bedeutungen haben:

Is that **your** mother, Tom?	(**deine** Mutter)
Is that **your** son, Mrs Mason?	(**Ihr** Sohn)
Is that **your** bike, Jenny and Kate?	(**euer** Fahrrad)

Neben diesen Formen kommt auch *its* vor. *Its* bezieht sich immer auf eine Sache:
This is our school. **Its** classrooms are very nice.
This is Tom's bike. **Its** saddle is new.

Training 1: Everybody has got something

Add the possessive determiners.
<u>*Example:*</u> Timmy has got a teddy. It's his teddy.

1. Tom's grandparents have got a farm.   It's _____

2. The Masons have got a flat.   _____

3. Mr and Mrs Mason have got a car.   _____

4. Tom has got a sister.   _____

5. Kate has got a brother.   _____

6. Timmy has got a lot of toys.   _____

7. Mike has got a camera.   _____

8. Jenny has got a boyfriend.   _____

Training 2: Timmy's "toys"

Baby brothers and baby sisters often "find" things that belong to other people. Timmy does, too. He has got a big collection of things.

Complete what Mum says:

1. What have you got here, Timmy? Let me see – an exercise book.

Look, Timmy, it's not _____ exercise-book, it's Kate's. It's _____ exercise-book.

2. Where have you got that from, Timmy? Kate's German book! How can Kate do German tests when you keep it under _____ bed? What will _____ teacher say?

3. What about these keys, Timmy? Aren't they Dad's keys? I think they are _____ keys.

4. And look, Timmy. This is not _____ picture book, it's Kate's. It was _____ birthday present from Tom. So you can't keep it.

5. Don't cry, Timmy. Look, you've got so many things: here's _____ teddy, here's _____ van, here's _____ telephone. So play with _____ things now.

Verwechsle nicht *you* mit *your*, *its* mit *it's*, *they* mit *their* und *they're* mit *there*!

Timmy, where are **you**?
Where is **your** teddy?

It's Tom's bike. **Its** saddle is new.   Are Tom and Mike **there**? No, they
It's got a new bell, too.   aren't. **They're** at school.

Where are **their** bikes?
They're over there.

1. *your, its, their* sind Possessivbegleiter. Sie stehen immer vor einem Substantiv.
2. *they* ist ein Pronomen und steht für ein Substantiv im Plural. *They're* ist die Kurzform von *they are*.
3. *there* (= da, dort/dahin, dorthin) steht entweder allein oder vor einer Form von *to be* (= es gibt).

Nach *there is* muß das Substantiv im Singular stehen; nach *there are* folgt ein Substantiv im Plural:
There is **a boy** over there and there are **some girls** there, too.

Training 3: Your room

Put in "you" or "your", then answer the questions.

1. What about _____ room? Do _____ like it?

2. Do _____ clean it or does _____ mother clean it?

3. What's in _____ room?

4. Is there anything under _____ bed?

5. Where do _____ keep _____ clothes?

6. Where do _____ do _____ homework?

7. Have _____ got a TV in _____ room?

8. Have _____ got posters and photos in _____ room, too?

Training 4: Tom's room.

Put in "its", "it's", "they", "their" or "there".

_____ are a lot of things in Tom's room. _____ are books and cassettes every-where. _____ are on the chairs, on his bed and on the floor. And _____ is something under his bed. What is it? _____ an old pullover. _____ are some socks under his bed, too. _____ are holes in them and _____ look dirty. And what's that on the wall? _____ are a lot of photos and posters on the wall over his bed. Look at that photo over_____. _____ a photo of Jenny. She is sitting on her bike. _____ not a new bike, but _____ handlebars and _____ saddle are new.

Die Demonstrativbegleiter

Look at **this** book. This isn't my book.

And what about **that** book over there?

Yes, it is. And what about **these** pencils? Aren't they your pencils?

No, they aren't. But give me **those** pencils over there. They may be my pencils.

This/these verweisen auf Dinge oder Personen, die in der Nähe des Sprechers sind; *that/those* verweisen dagegen auf Dinge oder Personen, die weiter entfernt sind.

Ob du *this/that* oder *these/those* gebrauchen mußt, hängt von dem nachfolgenden Substantiv ab. Steht das Substantiv im Singular, steht immer *this/that*; steht das Substantiv im Plural, steht immer *these/those*.

This is my book and **that** is your book.
These are my pencils and **those** are your pencils.

Training 5: Timmy at school

Today Mrs Mason must see a doctor and Mr Mason can't stay at home, so Tom takes Timmy to school. Timmy wants to know everything.

Put in "this" or "that".

Timmy: Is _____ your classroom, Tom?

  Tom: No Timmy, _____ isn't my classroom. My classroom is over there.

Timmy: Is _____ your class, Tom?

  Tom: Yes, _____ is my class.

Timmy: And _____ class over there?

  Tom: _____'s Kate's class.

Timmy: Is _____ your chair here?

  Tom: Yes, it is. And look, Timmy, _____ chair over there, _____'s Jenny's.

Timmy: What's the name of _____ fat boy over there, Tommy?

  Tom: His name is John, but don't call him fat because he doesn't like it.

Timmy: Is _____ a teacher over there, Tom?

  Tom: No, it isn't. It's a pupil, Timmy.

Timmy: But _____ is a teacher, Tom.

  Tom: Where? Over there? Ah yes, _____'s our English teacher. You're right, Timmy.

Timmy: And the girl beside him is his daughter?

  Tom: No, Timmy, it isn't. _____'s a girl in Kate's class.

Training 6: No, Timmy …

Timmy has collected a lot of things again, but Kate and Tom don't let him have everything.

<u>*Example:*</u> No, Timmy, this isn't your picture book. It's Kate's.
            Look! Your picture book is over there.

Go on. Use the following nouns:

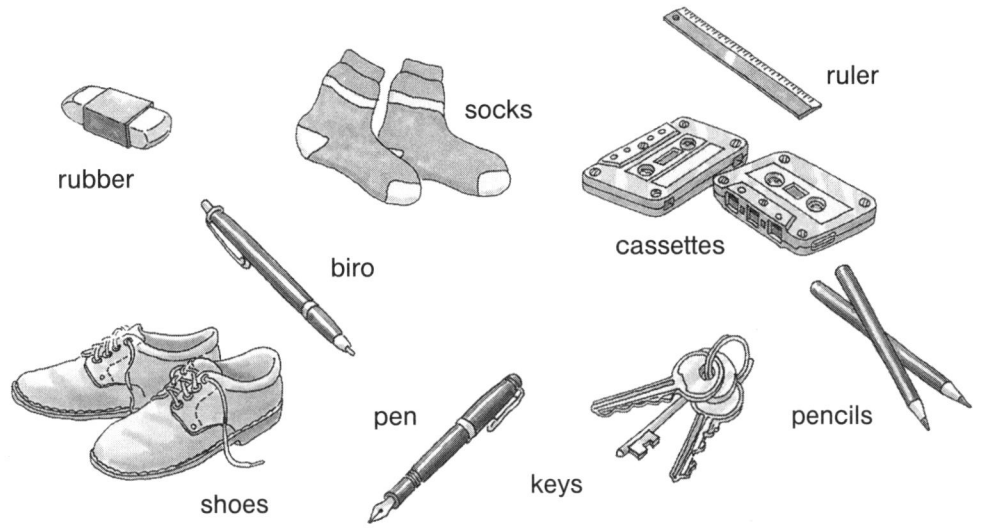

rubber

socks

ruler

biro

cassettes

pen

keys

shoes

pencils

Much und many

Zu den Begleitern zählen auch *much* und *many.* Beide entsprechen, wenn sie vor einem Substantiv stehen, dem Deutschen „viel(e)".

What about your class? Are there **many** girls in it? How **many** teachers have you got?

Many kann nur bei einem Substantiv im Plural stehen.

How **much** homework do you get? Is it too **much** or just right? How **much** time do you spend on your homework?

Much steht nur bei einem Substantiv im Singular.

Do you like English very **much**?

Bezieht sich *much* auf ein Verb, so bedeutet es meistens „sehr".

Training 7: A questionnaire

Put in "much" or "many".

1. How _____ homework have you got today?

2. How _____ time do you usually spend on it?

3. How _____ minutes do you spend on your English homework?

4. How _____ hours do you spend in front of the TV?

5. How _____ subjects have you got?

6. How _____ help do you get from your parents?

7. How _____ tests do you have a year?

8. How _____ good marks did you get last year?

9. How _____ tests have you written this week?

10. How _____ money do you get for good marks?

Training 8: What's school?

Complete with "much" or "many".

Well, school is

too _____ tests.

too _____ bad marks.

too _____ questions.

too _____ teachers.

too _____ boring subjects.

too _____ homework.

too _____ time indoors.

too _____ work.

That's why I love school so _____.

The s- and the of-genitive

Der s- und der of-Genitiv

Der *s*-Genitiv

Der *s*-Genitiv steht im Englischen zumeist bei Personen. Wie *my, your* etc. gibt er an, wem etwas gehört oder wem etwas zuzuordnen ist.
Seine Formen sind:

Singular: … 's
Kate**'s** book
a child**'s** voice

Regelmäßiger Plural:… s'
the girl**s'** books
my parent**s'** house

Unregelmäßiger Plural: … 's
children**'s** voices
people**'s** ideas

Verwechsle den *s*-Genitiv nicht mit dem Plural -*s*. Beim Plural steht nie ein Apostroph!
My parents are not at home.

Auch bei der 3. Person Einzahl im *simple present* steht nie ein Apostroph.
He works in an office.

Verwechsle den *s*-Genitiv auch nicht mit den Kurzformen von *is* und *has* (*'s*).

Training 1: The s-genitive

Write out the s-genitive forms.

Timmy/toys

Timmy's toys

the boys/teacher

_____

the girls/schoolbags

_____

our cat/food

_____

Kate/friends

_____

women/clothes

_____

the man/boots

_____

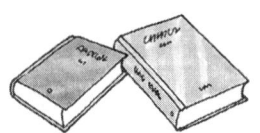

the children/books

_____

girls/school uniforms

_____

Jenny/dog

_____

the Masons/house

_____

my parents/car

_____

Training 2: A dialogue

Ask the questions and answer them.

	toys, Tom?	No,	(baby brother)
	girlfriend, Kevin?	No,	(Tom)
	magazine, Jenny?	No,	(the girls)
	cat, Kate?	No,	(my mother)
Is this your	homework, Joe?	No, they aren't. They are ...	(Kevin)
Are these your	house, Mr Mason?	No, it isn't. It's ...	(grandparents)
	your bike, Kate?	No,	(Jenny)
	your room, Tom?	No,	(my sister)
	your teddy, Jenny?	No,	(Timmy)
	your van, Timmy?	Yes, it is. It's my van!	

Training 3: Timmy's treasures

Put in the missing -s and the apostrophes.

Timmy is Tom__ baby brother. He is three years old. One of his favourite toy__ is

his teddy; but he__ got other toy__, too. He keeps them in his cupboard; but

there are other thing__ in his cupboard. Look! There__ one of Jenny__ letter__

to Tom; there__ an old German book and there__ Kate__ ruler. There are also

some key__; are they his parent__ key__? There__ a tennis ball, too. Whose is

it? Is it Kevin__or Joe__? It can't be Kate__ or Tom__ because they don't play

tennis.

Training 4: Jenny

The s-genitive or a short form? Mark with different colours.

Jenny is Tom's girlfriend. She's twelve. She hasn't got a brother or a sister; she's
only got her parents. Jenny is from York; her mother is from York, too, but her
father is from Nottingham. They live in an old house; it's her grandparents' house.
Jenny's other relatives live in London; she's got an aunt there who's over sixty
and who's got a flat in London. She hasn't got any children, so Jenny is her only
niece. In her summer holidays Jenny wants to see her: it will be Jenny's first visit
to London.

Der of-Genitiv

Der *of*-Genitiv (oft auch *of-phrase* genannt) drückt Zugehörigkeit und Mengenangaben aus. Im Unterschied zum *s*-Genitiv steht er meist nur bei Sachen.

the pages **of** a book   a bottle **of** lemonade
the legs **of** the table   a pound **of** apples

Zugehörigkeit   Mengenangaben

Training 5: The of- or the s-genitive?

Example: the boys' legs – the doors of my room

the boys/legs   the girl/hands   the car/windows

the doors/my room   the dog/feet   my neighbour/cat

Kate/books   the children/clothes   the end/school

on the evening/my birthday   the light/the moon   Jenny/story

Training 6: What goes together?

Example: a bar of chocolate

a bar	of	milk		a tin	of	cornflakes
lots	of	tea		a pound	of	crisps
a glass	of	food		a bag	of	cheese
a cup	of	strawberries		a packet	of	peas
a plate	of	chocolate		a piece	of	sausages

Training 7: Tom's shopping list

In a few days it's Tom's birthday. He wants to invite some friends and have a party.
The day before the party he goes with his friend Mike to Mrs White's corner shop to
buy some things. Here is his shopping list. Can you complete it?

five _____ crisps
three _____ biscuits
five _____ coke
five _____ lemonade
three _____ sausages
two _____ pineapples
five _____ ice cream

Tom takes some money **out of** his
purse.
The purse falls **off** the table. Hands
off! It's Tom's purse.

I've got a postcard **from** my father.
It's **from** London. There are greetings **from** all the family on it.

Sei vorsichtig. Der *of*-Genitiv wird oft
mit der Präposition *off* (von … her-
unter/weg) oder mit *out of* (aus/her-
aus) verwechselt.

Verwechsle den *of*- und den *s*-Geni-
tiv nicht mit der Präposition *from*. Die
Präposition *from* gibt meist eine
Richtung von einer Person oder von
einem Ort her an.

Training 8: The s-genitive, of, out of, off or from?

Complete the text.

"Get _____ that bike," Tom said to Mike, "Let's put all the things on it. Then we needn't carry them." So they put all their things on Tom _____ bike. "Be careful, Mike, hold the bottles or they will fall _____ the bike." So Mike took one hand _____ his pockets and tried to hold them. It was not very far _____ the corner shop to the Masons _____ flat – only a five minutes' walk. But soon there was a loud crash and the bottles fell _____ the bike. Two bottles _____ lemonade were broken. So they had to go back to Mrs White _____ shop. This time they got home all right. No bottles fell _____ the bike and Mike even took both hands _____ his pockets.

At home, they carried everything into the kitchen. Then they went upstairs into Tom _____ room and talked about the party. Five minutes later there was a tele-phone call _____ Jenny _____ mother. "Jenny is ill, Tom. She's just come home _____ school and she looks really ill. I'm afraid she can't come to your party. But I nearly forgot to wish you all the best for your birthday – greetings _____ Jenny and _____ my husband. You will hear _____ Jenny tomorrow. Bye, Tom, and have a nice party!"

Kapitel 6

The present of "have got"

Das Präsens von „haben"

Formen

Bejahte Formen		Verneinte Formen	
Langformen	Kurzformen	Langformen	Kurzformen
I have got	I've got	I have not got	I haven't got
you have got	you've got	you have not got	you haven't got
he **has** got	he**'s** got	he **has not** got	he **hasn't** got
she **has** got	she**'s** got	she **has not** got	she **hasn't** got
it **has** got	it**'s** got	it **has not** got	it **hasn't** got
we have got	we've got	we have not got	we haven't got
you have got	you've got	you have not got	you haven't got
they have got	they've got	they havenot got	they haven't got

Bei *haven't* fällt das **-e** nicht aus. Der Apostroph steht nur für ein ausgefallenes **-o**. Bei *has* steht nie ein **-e**.

Ob du *have got* oder *has got* gebrauchen mußt, hängt vom Subjekt ab:

| **Kate** | **has got** | a bike. |
| **My friends** | **have got** | bikes, too. |

Training 1: The Masons' house

Put in the correct forms of "have got".

1. Tom's parents live in York. They _____ a flat there.

2. They _____ five rooms.

3. Tom _____ a room, and Kate _____ a room , too.

4. Timmy _____ a big room. His room is small.

5. The Masons _____ a car.

6. Tom and Kate _____ a car, they _____ bikes.

7. Timmy _____ a bike because he's too young.

8. But he _____ two big toy cars and other toys in his room.

Training 2: Timmy's toys

Timmy has got a cat, a dog, a teddy, two buckets, a telephone, some toy cars and two or three picture books.

a) Now you are Timmy. Tell your friends what you have got.
b) What about you? What have you got?

Training 3: What Kate has got

a) _Example:_ Kate has got two brothers, but she hasn't got a sister.

two brothers

boyfriend

bike

sister

a lot of friends

car

a teddy

a football

a radio

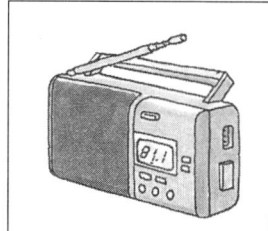

toy car

dog

TV

b) _What about you? – I have got … , but I haven't got …_
c) _What about your friend(s)? Have they got brothers, sisters, etc.?_

Fragen und Kurzantworten

Has	Kate	got	a brother?	Yes,	she	**has.**
Has	Kate	got	a sister?	No,	she	**hasn't.**
Have	her parents	got	a house?	No,	they	**haven't.**
Have	they	got	a flat?	Yes,	they	**have.**
has/have	Subjekt	Verb			Subjekt	Verb
					(Pronomen)	

Bei Fragen stehen *have/has* vor dem Subjekt. *Got* steht nach dem Subjekt.

Bei Kurzantworten mußt du das Subjekt als Pronomen wiederholen.
Nach *yes* steht eine bejahte Langform, nach *no* eine verneinte Kurzform.

Training 4: Kate

a) *Look at Training 3, then ask questions and give short answers.*

1. Has Kate got a brother?   Yes, she …
2. Has she got a sister?   No, she …

Go on.

b) *Ask Kate.*

Have you got a brother, Kate? Yes, I …

Go on.

Training 5: What about you?

Ask as many questions as you can and give short answers.

| Has Have | you your parents your friends your mother your grandmother your English teachers your boyfriend your father | got | a car a lot of toys a house a water-pistol an English book a toy car a potty a hamster | Yes, … No, … |

Kapitel 7

The present of "to be"

Das Präsens von „sein"

Formen

	Bejahte Formen		Verneinte Formen	
	Langformen	Kurzformen	Langformen	Kurzformen
	I **am**	I**'m**	I **am** not	I**'m not**
	you **are**	you**'re**	you **are** not	you **aren't**
	he **is**	he**'s**	he **is** not	he **isn't**
	she **is**	she**'s**	she **is** not	she **isn't**
	it **is**	it**'s**	it **is** not	it **isn't**
	we **are**	we**'re**	we **are** not	we **aren't**
	you **are**	you**'re**	you **are** not	you **aren't**
	they **are**	they**'re**	they **are** not	they **aren't**

Der Apostroph in den Kurzformen steht auch hier für einen ausgefallenen Vokal, z.B. für das *o* in *isn't/aren't*.

Auch bei *to be* richtet sich die Form des Verbs nach dem Subjekt:

I	**am**	ill.
They	**are**	my friends.

Training 1: Tom's birthday

Put in the right forms of "to be".

Today, it _____ Tom's birthday. He _____ twelve years old today. All his friends

_____ there. His sister _____ there, too. Her name _____ Kate. She _____

eleven years old. Only Jenny, his girlfriend, _____ not there. Where _____ she?

She _____ ill. They _____ all in the kitchen; it _____ full of children. They _____ all hungry and thirsty. There _____ a lot of sandwiches on the table; there _____ some bottles of lemonade, too. But one bottle _____ on the floor; it _____ broken and there _____ a pool of lemonade around it. And who _____ in the pool? It _____ Timmy, Tom's baby brother.

Training 2: Tom's friends

Tom tells us everything about his friends and his family.

Complete the sentences with forms of "to be".

That _____ Kevin and that _____ Joe.

They _____ my best friends.

They _____ in my class.

And that boy over there _____ Bill. He

_____ in my class, too, and he _____

very good at maths. In tests he can

_____ very useful!

And that girl over there? That _____ my sister! Her name

_____ Kate. All her teachers _____ very happy when she

_____ ill! And I _____ happy when she _____ back at

school again!

And this _____ my baby brother.

His name _____ Timmy.

He _____ three years old.

Fragen und Kurzantworten

Is	it	Tom's birthday?		Yes,	it	**is.**
Is	Jenny	there, too?		No,	she	**isn't.**
Is	she	ill?		Yes,	she	**is.**
Are	the children	hungry?		Yes,	they	**are.**
Are	there	sandwiches on the table?		Yes,	there	**are.**
Is	that	Tom's baby brother?		Yes,	it	**is.**

Verb   Subjekt   Subjekt   Verb
                                                                       (Pronomen)

- Bei Fragen mit *to be* steht das Verb vor dem Subjekt.
- Bei Fragen mit *is there/are there* ist *there* gleichsam das Subjekt der Frage.

- Bei Kurzantworten (Antworten, die sich im Deutschen auf ja oder nein beschränken) mußt du das Subjekt als Pronomen wiederholen.
- Bei einer Antwort mit *yes* steht das Verb in der Langform, bei *no* in der Kurzform.
- Auf die Frage *is that* antwortet man mit *Yes, it is/No, it isn't*, auch wenn nach Personen gefragt wird.

Training 3: Your answers

Read through Training 1 on page 39 again. Then give short answers.

1. Is it Timmy's birthday?
2. Is Jenny there?
3. Is Tom eleven years old?
4. Is Jenny Tom's mother?
5. Is Kate Tom's sister?
6. Is that Timmy in the lemonade?
7. Are there sandwiches on the table?
8. Are the children in the bathroom?
9. Are they hungry and thirsty?
10. Is one bottle on the floor?

Go on with other questions and answers.

Training 4: A game

At Tom's party the children play a game. They must ask questions and find out what "it" is.

Answer their questions.

Is it a thing?	No, _____
Is it an animal?	No, _____
Is it in this room?	No, _____
Is it a toy?	No, _____
Is it something nice?	No, _____
Is it something terrible?	Yes, _____
Is it a woman?	No, _____
Is it a man?	Yes, _____
Is he old?	Yes, _____
Is he at our school?	Yes, _____
Is it a teacher?	Yes, _____
Is it our maths teacher?	Yes, it is.

Fragen mit what, who, where, why und how

Who is Jenny? **Who's** that?	**who** (= wer) fragt nach Personen.
What is on the table? **What's** that?	**what** (= was) fragt nach Sachen.
Where is Jenny? **Where's** she from? **Where** are you, Timmy?	**where** (= wo) fragt nach einem Ort.
Why isn't Jenny here?	**Why** (= warum) fragt nach dem Grund.
How old is she ?	**How** (= wie) fragt in Verbindung mit *old* nach dem Alter.

Training 5: Jenny

At the party, Mike wants to know all about Jenny. He asks Tom a lot of questions.
He wants to know

- who Jenny is
- how old she is
- if she is a nice girl
- why she isn't here
- where she is now

- if her parents are at home
- what she has got
- if she has got a temperature
- if she has got brothers and sisters
- if she is from York

Ask Mike's questions.

Training 6: Tom's answers

Here are some of Tom's answers. What are the questions?

1. _____
   No, she isn't. She's twelve.

2. _____
   Yes, she is. She's a very nice girl.

3. _____
   Yes, she is. She's my girlfriend.

4. _____
   Because she's ill.

5. _____
   She's got a cold.

6. _____
   No, she hasn't. She hasn't got a temperature.

7. _____
   She's at home.

8. _____
   Her parents are at home, too.

9. _____
   No, I'm not. But I'm sorry that she isn't here.

The present progressive

Die Verlaufsform des Präsens

Formen

Bejahte Formen

Langformen		Kurzformen	
I **am**	talk**ing**	I**'m**	talk**ing**
you **are**	talk**ing**	you**'re**	talk**ing**
he **is**	talk**ing**	he**'s**	talk**ing**
she **is**	talk**ing**	she**'s**	talk**ing**
it **is**	talk**ing**	it**'s**	talk**ing**
we **are**	talk**ing**	we**'re**	talk**ing**
you **are**	talk**ing**	you**'re**	talk**ing**
they **are**	talk**ing**	they**'re**	talk**ing**

Verneinte Formen

Langformen		Kurzformen	
I **am not**	talk**ing**	I**'m not**	talk**ing**
you **are not**	talk**ing**	you **aren't**	talk**ing**
he **is not**	talk**ing**	he **isn't**	talk**ing**
she **is not**	talk**ing**	she **isn't**	talk**ing**
it **is not**	talk**ing**	it **isn't**	talk**ing**
we **are not**	talk**ing**	we **aren't**	talk**ing**
you **are not**	talk**ing**	you **aren't**	talk**ing**
they **are not**	talk**ing**	they **aren't**	talk**ing**

• Das *present progressive* wird mit den Formen von *to be* und einer *ing*-form, dem *present participle* (= Partizip Präsens) gebildet. Das *present progressive* besteht daher immer aus zwei Teilen.

- Das *present participle* wird mit dem Infinitiv + *ing* gebildet. Beachte allerdings bei der Bildung:

come + ing	co**m**ing	Ein auslautendes -*e*, das nicht gesprochen wird, entfällt.
sit + ing	si**tt**ing	Bei einsilbigen Verben mit kurzem, betontem Vokal wird der auslautende
swim + ing	swi**mm**ing	Konsonant verdoppelt.
lie + ing	l**y**ing	*ie* wird vor folgendem -*ing* zu *y*.

- Auch bei dem *present progressive* – wie bei allen Zeitformen – bestimmt das Subjekt die Form von *to be*, die du gebrauchen mußt.

Training 1: Present participles

Form the present participles.

come	*coming*	make	
lie		get	
dry		play	
call		put	
cut		run	
dance		sit	
drink		swim	
fly		tie	
listen		watch	

Training 2: At Tom's party

At Tom's party all the children are busy. What are they doing?

1. Mike/take/photos.
2. John/sit at the kitchen table/and drink/all the lemonade.
3. Kate/skip.
4. Tom/ring up/Jenny.
5. Betty/flirt/with Kevin.
6. Some boys/play/football in the kitchen.
7. Some girls/dance/in the kitchen.
8. Ann/lie on the floor/and watch/a film on TV.
9. Jim and Barbara/eat/sandwiches.
10. Susan/sit in a corner/and read/a magazine.

Training 3: Timmy's "report"

Timmy is at the party, too, but he's very small and Tom doesn't want to have him there. So he tells him to go to his mother. Timmy goes and tells his mum that

1. Mike is playing with his camera.
2. John is eating all the sandwiches.
3. Kate is hopping around like a rabbit.
4. Tom is talking to his teacher.
5. Betty is talking nonsense to Kevin.
6. some boys are quarrelling about a ball.
7. some girls are running around in the kitchen.
8. Ann is lying on the floor because she is ill.
9. Jim and Barbara are making sandwiches.
10. Susan is reading my picture book.

Can you correct Timmy?

<u>*Example:*</u> That's not right, Timmy. Mike isn't playing with his camera, he's taking photos.

Fragen und Kurzantworten

Are	you	talk**ing**	to your teacher?
Is	Jenny	ly**ing**	in bed?
What	**are**	you	do**ing**, Tom?

- Bei Fragen im *present progressive* steht zunächst eine Form von *to be*, dann das Subjekt und schließlich das *present participle*.
- Fragewörter wie *why, where, when, what* werden einfach vor die Form von *to be* gesetzt. Die Wortstellung ändert sich dadurch nicht.

No,	I'	**m not.**	Pronomen + Kurzform (verneinte Form)
Yes,	I	**am.**	Pronomen + Langform (bejahte Form)
Yes,	she	**is.**	
No,	she	**isn't.**	

- Bei den Kurzantworten wird das *present participle* ausgelassen. Ansonsten gelten die bereits bekannten Regeln.
- Bei Fragen mit Fragewörtern sind keine Kurzantworten möglich.
  What are you doing, Tom? I'm talking to Jenny.

Training 4: Timmy's questions

When Timmy's mother hears what Timmy says, she thinks that he is wrong. So she asks him some questions. Ask her questions and give Timmy's answers.

<u>*Example:*</u> Is Mike really playing with his camera? – Yes, he is.
          Is John really eating all the sandwiches? …

          Go on.

Training 5: Timmy's questions

Timmy's mother still thinks that he's wrong, so she sends him back. She wants to know

 – what Kate is doing,
 – if Tom is really talking to his teacher,
 – what Mike is doing with his camera,
 – if Susan is really reading his picture book,
 – why Ann is lying on the floor,
 – if Kate is playing a new game,
 – what the boys are doing with the ball,
 – what the girls are doing in the kitchen,
 – what John is doing,
 – what Jim and Barbara are doing.

Now you are Timmy. Ask Timmy's questions and give the answers.

<u>*Example:*</u> What are you doing, Kate? – I'm skipping.

Training 6: In Timmy's room

First scene:
At <u>7.30</u> the party is over. The children are going <u>home</u>. They are all <u>happy</u>. <u>Timmy</u> is happy, too. He is <u>in his room</u>. He is lying <u>on the floor</u>, but he isn't <u>crying</u>. <u>He's</u> playing with Tom's birthday presents. They are <u>in his room</u> now. One parcel is open. There's a picture book and some chocolate in it.

Second scene:
Timmy is still lying <u>on the floor</u>. There is chocolate on his face and hands. He isn't playing any more. He's got <u>a pencil</u> in his hand and he is drawing <u>a picture</u> in Tom's picture book.

Third scene:
<u>Somebody</u> is coming upstairs. He is shouting <u>a name</u>. It is Timmy's brother. He <u>is looking for</u> his presents. He is angry. He is opening the door of Timmy's room. But the room is empty. Where is Timmy? Can you see him?

Read through the text, then ask about the underlined words. Be careful with the question words. Remember:

who?	–	wer?
where?	–	wo, wohin?
what?	–	was?
when?	–	wann?
why?	–	warum, wieso?
how?	–	wie?

Modal auxiliaries

Modale Hilfsverben

After the party Kate <u>can</u> go to her room. It isn't her birthday, so she <u>needn't</u> help. But Tom <u>must.</u> He <u>must</u> help his mother to wash up the dishes and clean the kitchen floor. Then they <u>must</u> tidy up the living-room.

<u>Must</u> Timmy help, too? No, he <u>needn't.</u> He <u>must</u> go to bed because it's already late. He is very unhappy. "Why <u>can't</u> I help you? Why <u>must</u> I always go to bed?" he cries. "Look, Timmy," his mother says, "It's already 8 o'clock; you <u>must</u> go to bed now. You <u>can</u> stay up longer next year." But Timmy is still unhappy. "I <u>can</u> wash the dishes, too." "OK, Timmy, you <u>can</u> help Tom with the dishes, but you <u>mustn't</u> drop them," his mother says. "Fetch the dirty plates from the living-room," Tom says to him. Timmy is happy now. He is big and strong and he <u>can</u> help. But what's that? There is a loud noise in the living-room, then everything is quiet again. When Tom opens the door, Timmy is gone, but there are three plates on the floor …

Schau dir den Text genau an. Die unterstrichenen Verben sind sogenannte modale Hilfsverben.

 Modale Hilfsverben gibt es auch im Deutschen. Es entsprechen dabei:

can	können, dürfen
can't	nicht können, nicht dürfen
mustn't	nicht dürfen
must	müssen
needn't	nicht müssen, nicht brauchen

Für „dürfen" bzw. „nicht dürfen" kann in Fragen und Kurzantworten auch *may* (statt *can*) bzw. *may not* (statt *mustn't, can't*) stehen:

May I help you?

Yes, you **may.**

No, you **may not.**

Englische Hilfsverben weisen folgende Eigenschaften auf:

1. Sie haben keinen Infinitiv und kein -*s* in der 3. Person Singular.
2. Ihre Formen sind für alle Personen gleich.
3. Hilfsverben können im Englischen nicht alleine stehen; ihnen muß immer ein Verb folgen (eine Ausnahme bilden die Kurzantworten). Vergleiche:

Er **kann** English.   He **can speak** English.

4. Wie im Deutschen folgt einem Hilfsverb immer ein Infinitiv.
5. Objekte und andere Ergänzungen stehen im Englischen immer nach der Verbgruppe. Vergleiche:

Er **kann** sie sehen.   He **can see** her.

Training 1: Timmy

Complete the sentences.

Timmy is three.

1. He _____ go to school.	1. Er braucht nicht …
2. He _____ go to kindergarten.	2. Er kann …
3. He _____ play with other children there.	3. Er kann …
4. _____ he go there every day?	4. Muß er …?
5. No, he _____ .	5. Nein, er muß nicht.
6. _____ he go there alone?	6. Darf er …?
7. No, he _____ .	7. Nein, er darf nicht.
8. _____ he take his bike?	8. Darf er …?
9. No, he _____ . It's too dangerous.	9. Nein, er darf nicht.
10. _____ Tom fetch him in the afternoon?	10. Muß Tom …
11. Yes, he _____ on Thursdays and Fridays.	11. Ja, er muß …

Training 2: Right or wrong?

Look at the text again, then correct the wrong statements.

1. Kate must go to her room. – No, that's wrong. Kate can go to her room.

> 1. Kate must go to her room.
> 2. She mustn't help her mother.
> 3. Tom must clean Kate's room.
> 4. He needn't wash up the dishes.
> 5. He must clean the kitchen floor.
> 6. He must clean the kitchen windows, too.
> 7. Timmy can help him.
> 8. Timmy must clean the kitchen floor, too.
> 9. Timmy must drop the plates.
> 10. Timmy can stay up a little longer.

Training 3: A phone call

The next day, Tom rings up Jenny again. Jenny's mother answers the phone.

Tom	Jenny's mother
1. _____ I talk to Jenny, please?	1. Sorry, Tom, you _____ Jenny's in the bathroom.
2. _____ Jenny come to school tomorrow?	2. No, she _____ . She _____ get up.
3. _____ she stay in bed all day?	3. Yes, she _____ .
4. _____ she take medicine?	4. No, she _____ .
5. _____ I see her this afternoon?	5. No, you _____ see her today. She _____ go to the doctor's.

Training 4: What Jenny must do

When Tom rings up again, Jenny tells him what she must or mustn't do.

Begin: I must/mustn't …

2. Stay in bed.

3. Don't watch too much TV.

1. Don't go to school.

4. Take your temperature every morning.

5. Take your medicine.

6. Come to my surgery again on Monday at 4 o'clock.

7. Don't play with your friends.

Training 5: Jenny is really ill

What can, must, needn't, mustn't Jenny do?

take her medicine   watch TV

ride her bike   read a book

go to school   clean her room

do her homework   help her mother in the kitchen

ring up her friends   listen to music

write letters   play football

Training 6: Good patients

Correct the following statements. One sentence is already correct.

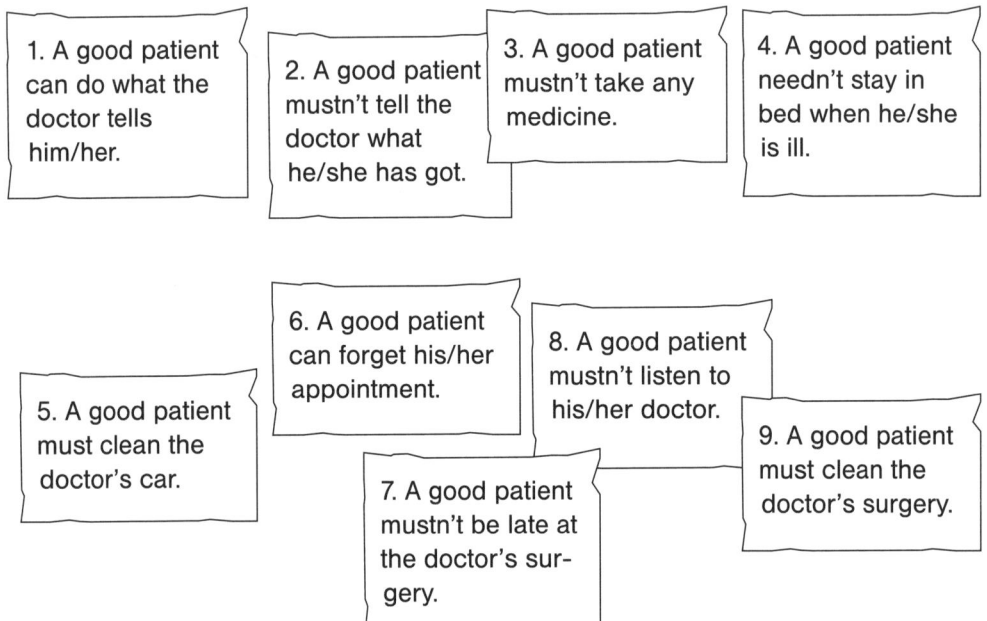

1. A good patient can do what the doctor tells him/her.

2. A good patient mustn't tell the doctor what he/she has got.

3. A good patient mustn't take any medicine.

4. A good patient needn't stay in bed when he/she is ill.

5. A good patient must clean the doctor's car.

6. A good patient can forget his/her appointment.

7. A good patient mustn't be late at the doctor's surgery.

8. A good patient mustn't listen to his/her doctor.

9. A good patient must clean the doctor's surgery.

Fragen und Kurzantworten

Can	Kate	get up?	Yes,	she	**can.**
			No,	she	**can't.**
Must	she	stay in bed?	Yes,	she	**must.**
			No,	she	**needn't.**
Hilfsverb	Subj.	Infinitiv		Pronomen	Hilfsverb

Bei Fragen steht das Hilfsverb vor dem Subjekt; nach dem Subjekt steht immer der Infinitiv.
Bei Kurzfragen wird nur das Hilfsverb wiederholt; die verneinte Form von *must* ist *needn't*.

Training 7: At the doctor's

When you are ill, you can ask your doctor a lot of questions. Can you give the doctor's answers?

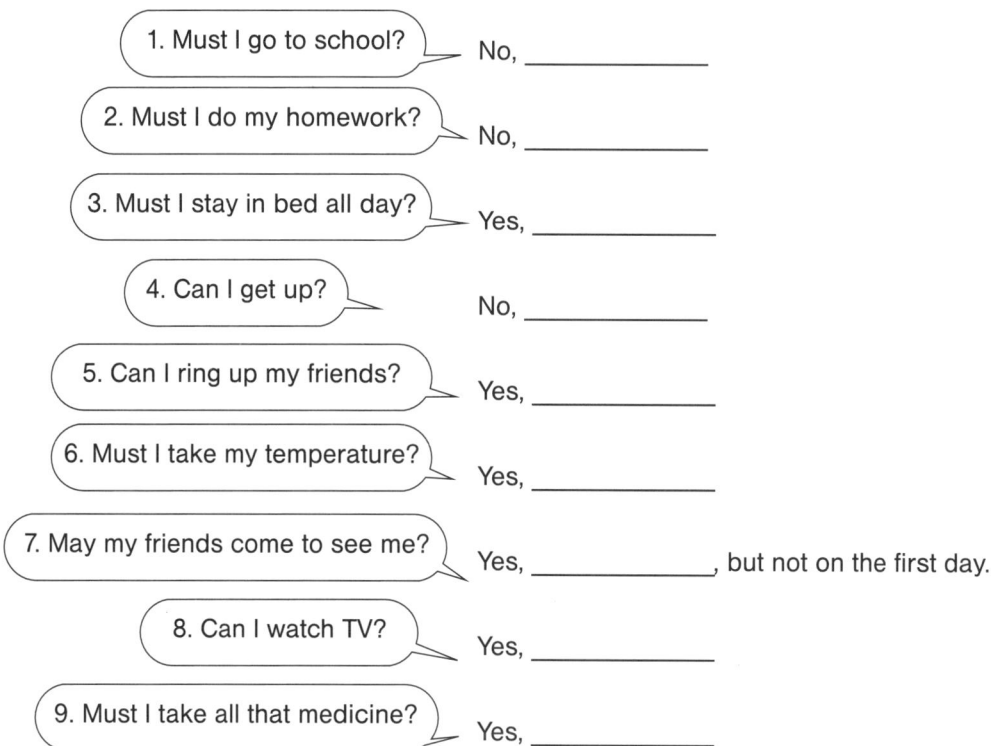

1. Must I go to school?   No, _____

2. Must I do my homework?   No, _____

3. Must I stay in bed all day?   Yes, _____

4. Can I get up?   No, _____

5. Can I ring up my friends?   Yes, _____

6. Must I take my temperature?   Yes, _____

7. May my friends come to see me?   Yes, _____, but not on the first day.

8. Can I watch TV?   Yes, _____

9. Must I take all that medicine?   Yes, _____

Training 8: Your questions

One of your friends is ill. You go and see her and you ask her

- if she is very ill   (Yes)
- if she must stay in bed   (Yes)
- if she must stay indoors all day   (Yes)
- if she may get up for an hour or two   (Yes)
- if she has got a temperature   (Yes)
- if she can go to school on Thursday   (No)
- if she is happy that she needn't go to school   (Yes)
- if her teachers are happy, too   (No)

Ask the questions and answer them.

Shall I ...? / Shall we ...?

Shall	I	open	the window for you?	Soll ich ...?
Shall	I	give	you your medicine?	Soll ich ...?
Shall	we	call	the doctor again?	Sollen wir...?

Shall + Subj. + Infinitiv

Zu den modalen Hilfsverben gehört auch *shall*. Mit *Shall I / Shall we ...?* kann man einen Wunsch erfragen oder ein Angebot machen. Allerdings ist dies nur mit *I* und *we* möglich.

Training 9: Helping people

Your mother is ill. What can you do for her? Here are some ideas:

<u>Example:</u> Shall I do the shopping for you?

do the washing-up

do the shopping

clean the rooms

make her bed

go to the chemist's

make her some tea

get her medicine

cook the meals

open the window

ring up the doctor

look after my sister/brother

The simple present

Das Präsens von Vollverben

Vollverben sind Verben, die eine Tätigkeit oder einen Zustand nennen oder beschreiben. Sie kommen im Englischen wie im Deutschen in verschiedenen Zeiten (= *tenses*) vor. Eine dieser Zeiten ist das *simple present*:

Bejahte Formen

I	like	ice cream.	
You	like	sweets.	
My father	like**s**	tennis.	• In der 3. Person Singular *(he, she, it)* wird ein *-s* angehängt.
My mother	like**s**	English.	
A cat	like**s**	mice.	
We	like	Tom.	• Bis auf die dritte Person Singular hat das Präsens damit die gleiche Form wie der Infinitiv (ohne *to*).
You	like	us.	
They	like	TV.	

 Besonderheiten bei der Schreibung

He always catch**es** the bus at six o'clock.	• Bei Verben, die auf einen Zischlaut enden, hängt man ein *-es* [ɪz] an, wenn sie nicht auf *-e* enden.
He sometimes miss**es** it.	
He go**es** home.	• Auch bei *to go* und *to do* wird in der 3. Person Singular ein *-es* angehängt.
He do**es** his homework.	
to fl**y** He fl**ies** to France.	• Wie bei der Pluralbildung der Substantive ändert sich das *-y* nach einem Vokal nicht; nach einem Konsonant wird es jedoch zu *-ies*.
to tr**y** He tr**ies** to be helpful.	
aber:	
to sta**y** He sta**ys** at home.	

Training 1: What Tom does

Use the simple present.

1. He _____ at 7 o'clock every morning.   (get up)

2. Then he _____ and _____   (wash/put)

   on his clothes.

3. Then he _____ down to the dining-room.   (go)

4. There he _____ breakfast.   (have)

5. Then he _____ for his schoolbag.   (look)

6. After that he _____ the house.   (leave)

7. Then he _____ to the bus stop.   (go)

8. He usually _____ the bus when it is cold.   (take)

9. He _____ at school at a quarter to nine.   (arrive)

Training 2: Before lessons begin

copy   run   do   write   play

talk   make   clean   eat

a) Complete the sentences with the verbs in the cloud.

1. Mike and Tom _____ football in the classroom.

2. Sam _____ his sandwiches.

3. Sandra _____ her English homework.

4. Anne _____ to Betty.

5. John _____ his homework from his neighbour.

6. Kevin _____ around in the classroom.

7. Bob and David _____ a lot of noise, too.

8. Pam _____ the board.

9. Jane and Sharon _____ letters.

b) What do you usually do before lessons begin? Write down five sentences.

Verneinte Formen

I	**don't**	like	maths.
You	**don't**	like	biology.
Tom	**doesn't**	like	maths.
Jenny	**doesn't**	like	English.
We	**don't**	like	our teacher.
You	**don't**	like	geography.
They	**don't**	like	their teacher.
Subjekt	don't/doesn't	Infinitiv (no -s !)	

Bei der Verneinung mußt du eine Form von *to do* gebrauchen. Diese Form lautet in der 3. Person Singular *doesn't* (= *does not*), in den anderen Personen *don't* (= *do not*). Das folgende Verb steht im Infinitiv; d. h. du darfst in der dritten Person kein *-s* oder *-es* anhängen.

 Ist *to do* ein Vollverb, so heißt die Verneinung *don't do/doesn't do*:

He **doesn't do** his homework.
They **don't do** their homework.

Training 3: A strange family

The Browns live in Tom's neighbourhood. They have got four children. Say what they don't do.

1. They *don't get up* in the morning.   (get up)

2. They _____ an early breakfast.   (have)

3. Mr Brown _____ his car.   (wash)

4. Mrs Brown _____ the cooking.   (do)

5. Often, their children _____ to school.   (go)

6. They _____ school.   (like)

7. Helen _____ her teachers.   (like)

8. She _____ her homework.   (do)

Training 4: People are different

Example: Tom likes bananas, but he doesn't like oranges.

Tom		Jenny + Kate		Timmy		Mike		The Browns	
bananas	+	volleyball	+	cornflakes	+	photos	+	work	–
oranges	–	tennis	–	tea	–	comics	–	sleeping	+
Jenny	+	sports	+	dogs	+	music	+	books	–
Ben	–	all sports	–	cats	–	singing	–	TV	+

Training 5: Over to you

What do you/your friends/your parents like? What don't you/don't they like?

Example: I like football, but my father doesn't. He likes tennis.

Go on. Write down five sentences.

Fragen und Kurzantworten

Do	you	like	football?		Yes, I	**do.**
					No, I	**don't.**

Does	your mother	like	football, too?		Yes, she	**does.**
					No, she	**doesn't.**

| Form von to do | Subjekt (no -s /-es) | Infinitiv | | | Pronomen | Form von to do |

Bei Fragen mit einem Vollverb mußt du immer eine Form von _to do_ gebrauchen. Wie bei der Verneinung steht das Verb im Infinitiv.

In der Kurzantwort steht für das Vollverb immer eine Form von _to do._

Do you always **do** your homework?
Do you often **do** it in the morning?

Yes, I **do.**
No, I **don't.**

Wenn _to do_ ein Vollverb ist, muß es auch bei Fragen wiederholt werden.

Training 6: Mike

Mike is new in Tom's class. The first day his new classmates ask him a lot of questions.

_____ you like it here?

_____ your mother like York?

_____ you like English?

_____ you like school?

_____ you play hockey?

_____ you go to school by bike?

_____ you like sports?

_____ your sister go to our school, too?

_____ you play an instrument?

_____ your father work in York?

Training 7: Can you ask the questions?

A reporter for the school magazine asks Mike a lot of questions, too. What are they?

1. _____? Yes, I really like it. It's a nice class.

2. _____? No, I don't like all subjects.

3. _____? No, I don't. I really don't like maths.

4. _____? No, I don't like all the teachers.

5. _____? No, I don't forget my homework very often.

6. _____? No, I don't come to school by bus, I come on my bike.

7. _____? No. In winter I take the bus.

8. _____? No, I don't play football.

9. _____? Yes. My parents live here, too.

10. _____? Yes. I usually do my homework in the afternoon.

Fragen mit Fragewörtern

When	does	Mike	get	up?
When	do	his parents	get	up?
What	do	they	do	then?
Why	does	Mike	get	up at 7?
How	does	his sister	go	to school?
When	do	his parents	take	him there?
What subjects	doesn't	he	like?	

Fragewort	Form von to do	Subjekt	Infinitiv

Die Wortstellung: *„Form von to do + Subjekt + Infinitiv"* bleibt auch dann erhalten, wenn die Frage mit einem Fragewort beginnt.

 To do muß wiederholt werden, wenn es ein Vollverb ist:

What **does** Mike **do** in the evenings?
What **do** you **do** at school?

Training 8: An interview

Ask your friend and give his/her answers.

1. Where/you/live?
2. When/get up/in the morning?
3. When/your mother/get up?
4. What/have/for breakfast?
5. Why/not like/cornflakes?
6. When/your parents/leave the house?
7. When/they/come home again?
8. How/get/to school?
9. Why/not take/the bus?
10. What/do/in the afternoon?
11. What games/do/like?
12. What/do/in the evening?
13. When/go/to bed?
14. When/switch off/the light?
15. When/your parents/go to bed?

Training 9: Mike's father

a) Can you make up an interview with Mike's father?

1. He gets up at 5.30 o'clock in the morning.

When _____ you _____?

2. He starts work at seven o'clock.   When _____?

3. He leaves his house at 6.30.   When _____?

4. He drives a school bus.   What _____?

5. He collects the children from the villages.

Who _____?

6. He takes them to school.   Where _____?

7. School starts at a quarter to nine.   When _____?

8. In the afternoon he fetches them from school.

When _____?

9. He takes them home again.   Where _____?

10. Then he cleans the bus.   What _____?

11. He often finds things in the bus.   What _____?

b) Write down what Mike's father does.

Begin like this: I get up at 5.30 because work …

Training 10: Mike

Ask about the underlined words. Use the correct question words.

Mike lives in York now. He likes his new school, but he doesn't like all his subjects. He goes to school by bike. In winter and when it rains, his mother drives him to school. The first lesson begins at 8.45, so he gets up at 7. He leaves the house at a quarter to eight and usually arrives at school at 8.30. He has lunch at school because his parents don't come home until the evening. After school he often goes to see Tom. They play games together until 6 or 7 o'clock or do their homework. Then Mike goes home.

The simple present and
the present progressive

Kapitel 11

Die einfache Gegenwart und die Verlaufsform im Vergleich

Present progressive	Simple present
Look! Mike **is doing** his homework.	He always **does** his homework after school.
He**'s doing** a German exercise now.	He **goes** to a comprehensive school.
Das *present progressive* gebraucht man für Handlungen, die zur Zeit des Sprechens noch nicht vorbei sind, sondern noch ablaufen.	Das *simple present* gebraucht man für wiederholte, gewohnheitsmäßige und lang andauernde Handlungen.
Signalwörter dafür sind: *now, at this moment, look, listen, today, this morning (afternoon, evening)* etc.	Signalwörter sind hier: *always, often, sometimes, never, usually, every day (week, month, year), in the morning (afternoon, evening)* etc. Die Signalwörter stehen meist vor dem Hauptverb.

Training 1: Things are different today

Use the simple present or the present progressive.

1. Mike usually _____ up at 7, but today he is

   still in bed. He _____ .

2. He usually _____ breakfast at 7. 30, but

   today he _____ in bed.

3. He often _____ little time to spend in the

   bathroom, but this morning he _____ a bath.

get
sleep
have
still – lie
have
take

4. He usually _____ on his school uniform, but   put

today he _____ his other clothes.   wear

5. He usually _____ lunch at school, but today   have

he _____ lunch at home.

6. Mike usually _____ his mother with the   help

dishes, but today he needn't.

His father _____ the dishes.   wash

7. His parents usually _____ in the afternoon,   work

but things are different today. They _____ for   go

a walk. Do you know why?

Well, it's _____ .

Training 2: What about your Sundays?

What do you always/often/never/usually/sometimes do on Sundays?
Here are some ideas:

On Sundays I	always never usually sometimes often	get up late play football watch TV clean my bike clean my room ring up my friends cook lunch go for a walk help Mum und Dad brush my shoes do my homework learn English write letters go to school visit relatives listen to cassettes

Training 3: Mike's hobby

Use the simple present or the present progressive.

1. Mike _____ a picture of his new school. He   take

   _____ taking pictures.   like

2. He _____ only _____ pictures of   take

   schools, he _____ pictures of everything.

   Here he _____ a picture of Tom and Jenny.

3. He always _____ his pictures in an album.   put

   Look! He _____ a picture in his album now.

4. He _____ already _____ a lot of   have got

   albums. He _____ them in his room.   keep

Training 4: Mike's photos

Here are some of Mike's photos. Can you complete the text?

This is Dad.
sit/bus

This is Dad again.
clean/bus

This is our house.
live/there now

This is Mum.
leave the house/
always leave at 8

This is our garden.
Look! Mum/work in it/
like her garden

This is our corner shop.
Mum/work there/
sell groceries

Das simple present für aufeinanderfolgende Handlungen

After school Mike often goes to see Tom. When they arrive at Tom's, they first put their schoolbags in a corner. Then they go to the kitchen and look for something to drink. Then they go to Tom's room. There they play for an hour or two. After that they do their homework together. Then Mike goes home.

Das *simple present* steht im Englischen auch für aufeinanderfolgende Handlungen. Solche Handlungen kommen vor allem in Erzählungen und Berichten vor. Signalwörter sind *first, then, after that, next, soon, at last* etc.

Training 5: Scrambled eggs

Today Tom's and Kate's parents are out, but the children are very hungry. So they go into the kitchen and try to find something to eat. But the fridge is empty. There are only some eggs in it, so they try to make scrambled eggs. Connect the sentences and put them in the correct order. Use words like "first, now, then".

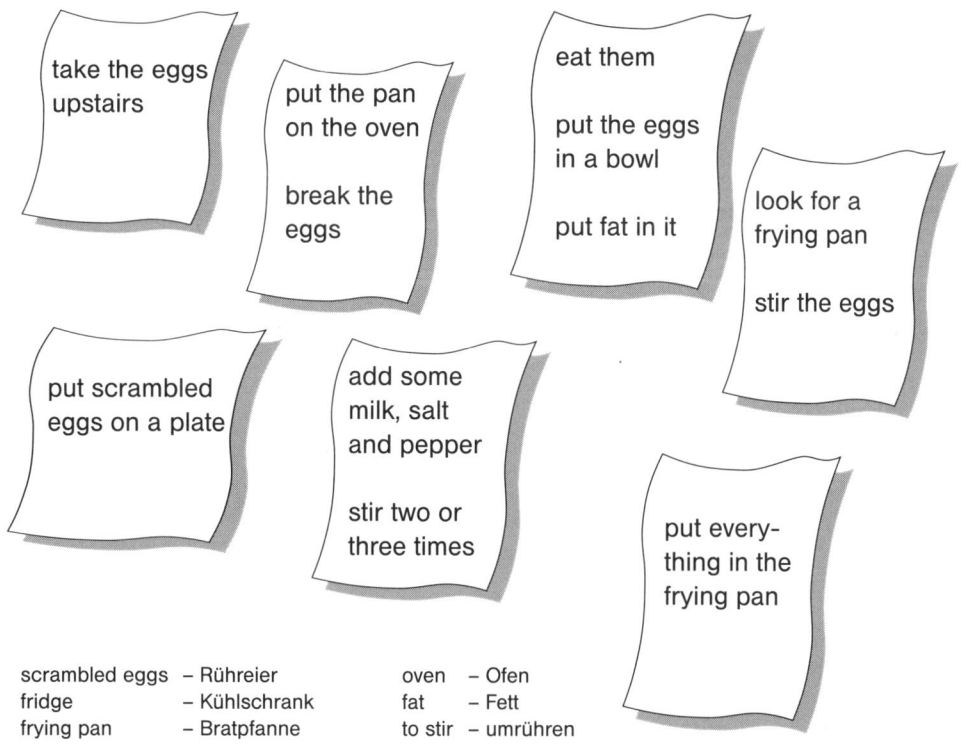

take the eggs upstairs

put the pan on the oven

break the eggs

eat them

put the eggs in a bowl

put fat in it

look for a frying pan

stir the eggs

put scrambled eggs on a plate

add some milk, salt and pepper

stir two or three times

put everything in the frying pan

scrambled eggs	– Rühreier	oven	– Ofen
fridge	– Kühlschrank	fat	– Fett
frying pan	– Bratpfanne	to stir	– umrühren

Training 6: Mr Mason

Usually Tom's and Kate's parents are home in the evening, but both work and so sometimes they are late. Tom's father is a vet. Here's a day in his life.

7^{00}	get up at seven o'clock
$7^{00} - 7^{30}$	wash
7^{30}	have breakfast
8^{00}	get in his car
8^{30}	open his surgery
$9^{00} - 12^{00}$	examine sick animals
12^{30}	have lunch at a restaurant
13^{45}	leave restaurant
17^{00}	have a cup of tea
17^{30}	close the door of the surgery
18^{00}	get home

a) Make up an interview. Ask Mr Mason what he usually does.

Example: When do you usually have breakfast?

b) Write down what Mr Mason does every day. Use signal words.

Training 7: What you do

Write about your day. Use signal words like first, then, etc.

Training 8: Another breakfast

Use the simple present or the present progressive.

The weather is fine and the sun _____ (shine). It is already ten

o'clock, and the Masons _____ still _____ (sit) at the

breakfast table. Nobody _____ (do) any work. Mr Mason

_____ (not look) after animals and Mrs Mason – she

_____ (work) in a hospital as a nurse – _____ (not look)

after her patients.

It's Sunday. The Masons always _____ (have) a late breakfast on

Sundays. But somebody is missing. It's Kate. She is still in her room; she

_____ (sleep). "Where's Kate?" Mr Mason _____ (ask).

"What _____ she _____ (do) in her room? Well, Timmy, go

and get her."

So Timmy _____ (go) to Kate's room. He _____ (open)

the door and _____ (see) that Kate is still in her bed. He

_____ (try) to wake her up, but Kate _____ (not listen), so

Timmy _____ (go) back and _____ (tell) his dad that Kate

_____ still _____ (sleep). "Haven't you got a water-pistol,

Tom?" Mr Mason _____ (say). "Come on, Timmy. Get it and ask your

sister if she _____ (not want) to get up now."

So Timmy _____ (fetch) Tom's water-pistol and _____ (go)

to Kate's room. Suddenly there is a loud noise in Kate's room and somebody

_____ (shout) in an angry voice: "Just you wait, Timmy!"

Questions, short answers
and negatives

Fragen, Kurzantworten und die Verneinung im Überblick

In the English lesson Tom sometimes writes letters to Jenny. Here is one of his letters, but somebody has changed it :

Dear Jenny,
I hope we **can't** see each other this afternoon. I have**n't** got a lot of homework to do, but I **don't** think I can come at 4 o'clock. Can you wait for me at the bus stop? I hope I **can't** come. I really **don't** want to see you again. You are**n't** the nicest girl I know. I am **not** always thinking of you. You know I **don't** like you.

Love, (ha! ha!)

Tom

Die Verneinung

Wenn du diesen Brief anschaust, siehst du, daß die Verneinung im Englischen nur bei Vollverben im *simple present* mit einer Form von *to do* (= *do not/does not* bzw. *don't/doesn't*) gebildet wird. Bei den Formen von *to be*, *have got*, den Hilfsverben *can, may* etc. und dem *present progressive* wird die Verneinung nur mit *not* gebildet.

Training 1: Tom's letter

Write Tom's letter again and correct it.

Training 2: What is right?

What do you think is right?

When Jenny gets Tom's letter,

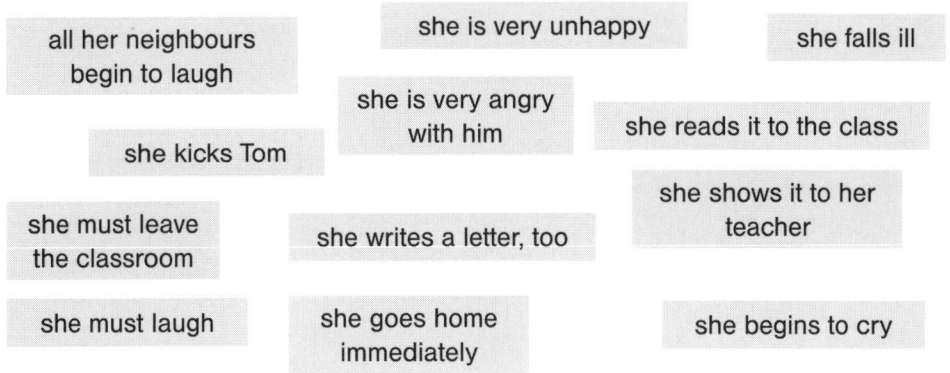

all her neighbours begin to laugh

she is very unhappy

she falls ill

she is very angry with him

she reads it to the class

she kicks Tom

she shows it to her teacher

she must leave the classroom

she writes a letter, too

she must laugh

she goes home immediately

she begins to cry

Example: Jenny doesn't begin to cry.

Training 3: Jenny

Make up Jenny's portrait.

Example: Jenny hasn't got a sister, but she has got a baby brother.

not a sister, a baby brother	Jenny – not ten, twelve years	her parents a flat, not a house	her father a van, not a car
to school not by bus, but by bike	like maths, not English	a good maths teacher, awful English teacher	not like all boys in her class, but Tom
sometimes late, but not often	like music, not like singing	can play a lot of games, but not football	good at volley-ball, bad at swimming

Training 4: Another portrait

Make up your own or a friend's portrait. Use negative forms, too.

Training 5: Good pupils

What's your idea of a good pupil? Here are some ideas to help you. Correct the sentences that are wrong. Use negative forms.

Good pupils always talk to their teachers.

Good pupils are silly.

Good pupils never forget anything.

Good pupils have got a lot of friends.

Good pupils never make their teachers angry.

Good pupils are unhappy.

Good pupils are bad at sports.

Good pupils never talk in lessons.

Good pupils work too much.

Good pupils always do their homework.

Die Fragebildung

Hilfsverb	Subjekt	Verb		Hilfsverb	Subjekt	Verb	
Does	Tom	**like** Jenny?	**Is**	Tom		happy?
Do	his parents	**like** her?	**Has**	he	**got**	a girlfriend?
			Is	he	**writing**	her a letter?
			Can	he	**see**	her?

Bei Fragen mit Formen von *to be, have got* oder Hilfsverben wie *can, must* etc. wird keine Form von *to do* gebraucht.

Auch im *present progressive* wird die Frageform nicht mit *to do* gebildet.

Training 6: An article for the school magazine

Tom is in his room. He is writing an article about pupils who are unhappy at school. He tries to make up a kind of test for his readers to see if they are happy or not. He wants to know if they

are often alone
like their parents
have got any friends
have got any hobbies
parents often play with them
have got anybody to talk to
watch a lot of TV
most of their teachers are nice
are often afraid
often cry
can do what they want
their parents are often out in the evening

Can you help Tom to ask the questions?

Example: Are you often alone?

Training 7: You and your school

Complete the sentences.

_____ you _____ school?			like
_____ you often _____ your homework?			forget
_____ you _____ your homework now?			do
_____ your mum _____ you now?			help
_____ your parents often _____ you?			help
_____ you _____ nice teachers?			have got
_____ they _____ you?			like

_____	they _____	you a lot of homework?	give
_____	you _____	during lessons?	can talk
_____	you _____	chewing gum in the English lessons?	may eat
_____	you _____	a school magazine at your school?	have got
_____	you _____	it?	read
_____	you _____	it interesting?	find

Training 8: Pupils, pupils …

As you know, there are different kinds of pupils. There are pupils who

– find everything boring
– often sleep during lessons
– are often late

– are often ill for tests
– only like sports

– can't sit still
– talk all the time
– can't listen

– listen only when the teacher gets angry
– often forget things
– don't do their homework

Find out what kind of pupil your friend is.
Make up a list of questions you can ask him/her.

Entscheidungsfragen und Kurzantworten

Bei Fragen mußt du zwischen zwei Grundtypen unterscheiden, nämlich zwischen Entscheidungsfragen und Ergänzungsfragen. Bei Entscheidungsfragen will man wissen, ob sich eine Sache so oder so verhält. Man antwortet daher immer mit ja oder nein. Im Englischen entspricht diesem ja oder nein eine Kurzantwort. Vergleiche:

to be	**Is**	Kate	ill?	Yes,	she	**is.**
				No,	she	**isn't.**
present progressive	**Is**	she	sleeping?	Yes,	she	**is.**
				No,	she	**isn't.**
auxiliary	**Must**	she	see a doctor?	Yes,	she	**must.**
				No,	she	**needn't.**
have got	**Has**	she	got a cold?	Yes,	she	**has.**
				No,	she	**hasn't.**
simple present	**Does**	she	go to school?	Yes,	she	**does**
				No,	she	**doesn't.**
	Do	her friends	look after her?	Yes,	they	**do.**
				No,	they	**don't.**
	Hv	S	Vb		S(Pron)	Hv

- Für Vollverben im *simple present* tritt eine Form von *to do* ein.
- Das Subjekt der Kurzantwort ist immer ein Pronomen (*I, you* etc.).
- Nach *yes* steht eine Langform, nach *no* die Kurzform.

| Is **this** your brother? | Yes, **it** is. |
| Is **that** your mother? | Yes, **it** is. |

Ist *this* oder *that* das Subjekt des Fragesatzes, so steht in der Kurzantwort immer *it*.

Training 9: Timmy's new picture book

While Tom is writing in his room, the door opens and Timmy comes in. He has got a new picture book and a lot of questions. Can you answer them? Give short answers.

1. Look at that house, Tom. Is that a church?
2. The man with the hat – is that a postman?
3. And what is he doing? Is he trying to get into the house?
4. And what about those men? Are they climbing the ladder?
5. Or are they running away?
6. Is the man running after the two other men?
7. Does he want to catch them?
8. Are they afraid of him?
9. Is he a policeman?
10. Do they want to steal the bike?
11. Do they want to ride away on it?
12. Is that a bike, too?

Ergänzungsfragen

Im Unterschied zu Entscheidungsfragen will man bei Ergänzungsfragen eine zusätzliche Information über eine Sache oder eine Person. Ergänzungsfragen beginnen daher immer mit einem Fragewort. Solche Fragewörter sind im Englischen:

who	(wer/wen)	fragt nach Personen
what	(was)	fragt nach Sachen
whose	(wessen)	fragt nach dem Besitzer
why	(warum)	fragt nach dem Grund
where	(wo/wohin)	fragt nach dem Ort oder der Richtung
when	(wann)	fragt nach der Zeit
how	(wie)	fragt nach dem Wie

Nach Ergänzungsfragen sind Kurzantworten mit *yes* oder *no* nicht möglich!

Bei Ergänzungsfragen mußt du beachten, ob du nach dem Subjekt eines Satzes oder nach anderen Satzteilen fragen willst.

a) Fragen nach dem Subjekt

Who	has got	a new pet?	**Jenny** has.
Who	must look	after it?	**Jenny** must.
Who	is looking	after it?	**Jenny** is.
Who	buys	its food?	**Jenny** does.
Who	doesn't pay	for its food?	**Jenny** doesn't.
Whose dad	pays	for it?	**Jenny's** dad does.
Subjekt			Subjekt

Bei der Frage nach dem Subjekt steht das Fragewort an der Stelle des Subjekts. *To do* wird deshalb nur in verneinten Fragen gebraucht. Diese Regeln gelten auch für das Fragepronomen *what,* wenn man nach dem Subjekt fragt (z. B. *What is lying on the table? What is happening?*).

Bei Fragen nach dem Subjekt steht das Verb – wie auch im Deutschen – immer in der 3. Person Singular:

Who is coming?
Who is ill?
Who has got a pet?

b) Fragen nach anderen Satzteilen

Bei Fragen nach anderen Satzteilen als dem Subjekt gelten die bereits bekannten Regeln:

Where	are	you?		Bei Fragen mit Formen von *to be*,
What	are	you	doing?	*have got* oder Hilfsverben wie *can,*
Who	are	you	ringing up?	*must* etc. wird keine Form von *to*
What	has	she	got?	*be* gebraucht. (Vgl. S. 72)
What	must	she	do?	
When	must	she	go?	
What	does	she	say?	*To do* ist nur bei Vollverben im
Who	does	she	help?	*simple present* möglich.
Where	does	she	go?	
Fragewort	Hv	S	Vb	

 Mit *who* (wer/wen) und *what* (was) kannst du sowohl nach dem Subjekt als auch nach dem Objekt fragen.

Who likes Tom? (= Wer mag Tom?)
Who does Tom like? (= Wen mag Tom?)

Training 10: Jenny

Ask about the underlined words.

1. <u>Jenny</u> is Tom's girlfriend.
2. <u>Her parents</u> are from Leeds.
3. They have got <u>a car</u>.
4. Sometimes <u>her parents</u> are strict (= streng).
5. She can't always see <u>Tom</u>.
6. She must tell her parents <u>where she is going</u>.
7. <u>She</u> must be back <u>early</u>.
8. She mustn't be out after 8 o'clock <u>in the evening</u>.
9. Listen! <u>The telephone</u> is ringing.
10. Tom is <u>at home</u>.

Training 11: A telephone call

Jenny wants to tell Tom some news, but the line is bad. So Tom must ask a lot of questions.

Example: Jenny: "I've got a new pet."   Tom: "What have you got?"

1. "I've got a new pet."	1. "What _____?"
2. "A new pet. It's a hamster."	2. "What _____?"
3. "I like it."	3. "What _____?"
4. "I must buy some food for it."	4. "What _____?"
5. " Food. Can you come to the pet shop?"	5. "Where _____?"
6. "Can you lend me some money?"	6. "What must _____?"
7. "I want to buy a book about hamsters, too."	7. "What _____?"
8. "A book about hamsters. I don't know anything about hamsters."	8. "I can't understand you. The line is very bad."
9. " _____?"	9. "The line. I can't understand you."
10. " _____?"	10. "You. Let's meet at the pet shop then."
11. "At the pet shop? Yes, OK, at three o'clock."	11. "OK. See you then."

Training 12: Bingo

Jenny and Tom meet at the pet shop. They buy a book and some food for Jenny's new pet. Then they go for a walk in the park. There they see two girls and a man with a dog. His name is Bingo.

The girls ask the man a lot of questions about the dog. Here are the man's answers. What are their questions?

1. How old _____? He's nearly two years old.

2. Where _____? He sleeps in the hall.

3. When _____? I usually get up at six.

4. What _____? Then I make him his breakfast.

5. What _____? Usually, he has some dog food.

6. When _____? Well, I take him for a walk after breakfast.

7. When _____? I go to work at half past eight.

8. Where _____? I take him to my neighbour's house.

9. How long _____? He stays there until I come home.

10. Where _____? We play in the garden.

11. What _____? I try to teach him some tricks.

12. What _____? In the evening? Well, we watch TV together.

13. What films _____? He likes westerns.

14. Why _____? Well, he likes horses.

Training 13: Making a date

Before Tom and Jenny go home again, they try to make a date. What are Tom's questions?

Where?   **What?**

Why?   **How long?**

When?

1. can see/again/you/I
2. we/meet again/can
3. you/stay/can
4. must/back/be/you
5. back/be/you/so early/must
6. must/your mother/help/you
7. must/do/you

The will- and going to-future

Das will- und going to-Futur

Das will-future

What **will happen** next year?	Kate **will** be twelve.
When **will** she **be** twelve?	Sh**e'll be** twelve in May.
Will she **be** happy then?	Yes, she **will.**
Will she **be** unhappy?	No, she **won't.**

Das *will-future* wird mit *will + Infinitiv* (bei Kurzformen: mit *'ll + Infinitiv*) gebildet. Verneinte Formen bildet man mit *will not + Infinitiv* (Kurzform: *won't + Infinitiv*), Fragen durch Umstellung von Subjekt und Prädikat. Bei Kurzantworten wird nur *will* bzw. *won't* wiederholt.

 Eine Form von *to do* ist bei *will* nicht möglich.

Training 1: An excursion

Kate's class is going on an excursion to the seaside. Complete what Mr Benson, her English teacher, tells them before they go.

I hope/water not too cold

I think/the weather be nice

If the water isn't too cold/we go for a swim

I hope/we spend a nice day together

We/spend the afternoon there

I don't think/it rain again

Perhaps the sun/shine

I hope/you have a good time

Training 2: Questions

a) The children have got a lot of questions. Ask their questions.
b) Imagine you are Mr Benson. What can you answer?

Jenny:
   when we be there?
   we need a warm pullover?
   you buy us an ice cream?

Kevin:
   lunch on the beach?
   play games on the beach?

Peter:
   what games we play?
   we be allowed to walk around
   on our own?

Susan:
   have time enough to go shopping?
   when we be back?
   the maths teacher come with us?

Der Gebrauch des will-future

Das *will*-Futur gebraucht man

1. Kate will be twelve in May.
   All her friends will come.

1. für zukünftige Handlungen, die nicht vom persönlichen Wollen oder persönlichen Wünschen, sondern von äußeren Umständen abhängen

2. I hope the weather will be nice.
   Perhaps she'll have a big party, too.
   I think I'll go.

2. für Vorhersagen und Vermutungen und um eine Hoffnung auszudrücken. Dies ist besonders nach *perhaps* und Verben wie *I think, I believe, I'm sure, I hope* der Fall

3. "I must buy a present for her."–
   "Oh, then I'll buy her a present, too."

3. bei spontanen Entschlüssen

4. If you go to her party, I'll go, too.
   But I'll go only if she invites me.

   When I see her, I'll ask her.
   I'll tell you when we see each other again.

4. im Hauptsatz von Bedingungssätzen und

   im Hauptsatz von Nebensätzen der Zeit

Training 3: Kate's hopes

Kate is looking forward to the excursion. This is what she hopes:

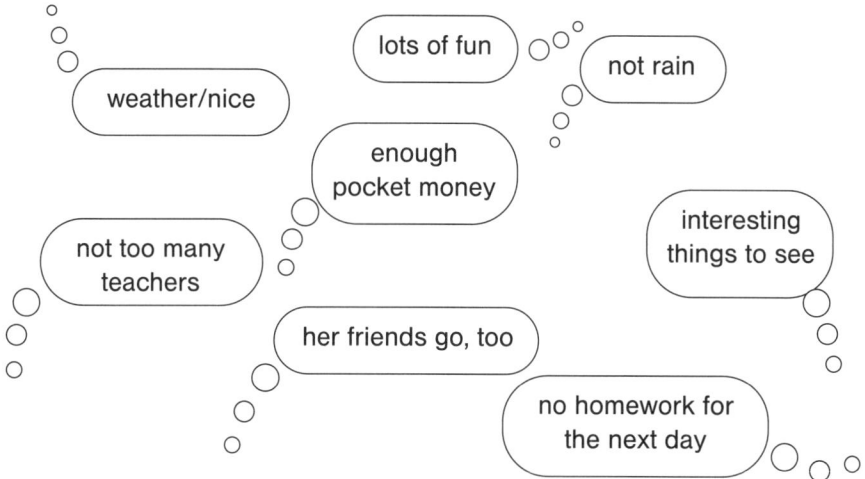

weather/nice

lots of fun

not rain

enough pocket money

not too many teachers

interesting things to see

her friends go, too

no homework for the next day

a) Form sentences. Begin with: She hopes, thinks, she's sure, perhaps, etc.
b) What about you? What do you hope when you go on an excursion?

Training 4: If …

What will happen		
	if the coach is late?	their teacher will be angry.
	if the coach breaks down?	they will be late.
	if it rains all day?	they won't leave at 8 o'clock.
	if the sun doesn't shine?	they won't go to the beach.
	if some of the children are late?	the driver won't be happy.
	if Mr Benson is ill?	there will be no excursion.
	if Kate loses her pocket money?	they won't go for a swim.
	if they take the wrong road?	she will be unhappy.

Example: If the coach is late, they won't leave at 8 o'clock.

Training 5: On the beach

Well, nobody is late and the bus doesn't have a breakdown. First they visit the old town, then they go to the beach. What will they do there? Here are some ideas:

When they are
on the beach,

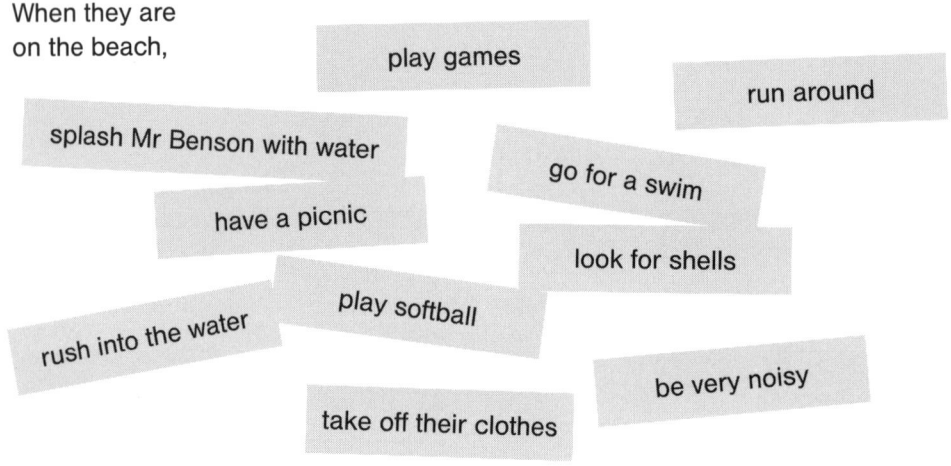

play games

run around

splash Mr Benson with water

go for a swim

have a picnic

look for shells

play softball

rush into the water

be very noisy

take off their clothes

splash – bespritzen; shell – Muschel

Training 6: There are nice people …

Before they go down to the beach, they walk around the old town and talk to each other. Complete what they say.

Jane: Look at these postcards. I need some.

Helen: _____

Kate: My bag is very
heavy. There are too
many things in it.
Ben: I'll carry it for you.

Christine: I must buy
something to drink.

Catherine: _____

Susan: I can't open this
bottle.
Jim: No problem.

_____

Kevin: I'm so hungry. I
think I'll have a sand-
wich.
Ronny: Well, then,

_____

Das going to-Futur

Wie du dich erinnerst, gibt es im Englischen noch ein weiteres Futur, nämlich das *going to*-Futur. Es wird mit dem Präsens von *to be* + *going to* gebildet. Dem *to* folgt ein Infinitiv. Verneinte Formen werden mit *not* gebildet, Fragen durch Umstellung von Subjekt und Prädikat.

"What **are** you **going to** do on your birthday, Kate?"
"I**'m going to** have a party and I**'m going to** invite all my friends."
"**Are you going to** invite Ben, too?"
"Yes, I am."
"And what about Ronny? **Are you going to** invite him, too?"
"No, I'm not. I**'m not going to** invite him."

Wenn du ausdrücken willst, daß jemand etwas in der Zukunft plant oder tun
will, mußt du das *going to*-Futur gebrauchen. Dies gilt vor allem dann, wenn
diese Absicht schon länger bestand.

 Verwechsle das *going to*-Futur nicht mit dem *present progressive*:

He**'s going** home.   He**'s going to go** home.
(Er geht gerade nach Hause.)   (Er hat vor, nach Hause zu gehen.)

Training 7: Plans, plans, plans …

Everybody has got plans, so Kate and her friends have got plans, too.
a) Complete the sentences with the going to-future.

help	go	invite	write
spend	clean	buy	work

1. Kate's tests aren't very good, so she _____ harder.

2. Jenny thinks that Kate's tests aren't very nice, so _____ .

3. Kate doesn't like Ronny, so she isn't _____ .

4. Helen likes Ben. She _____ this afternoon.

5. Linda's bike is very old. Her parents _____ .

6. Betty's room is very dirty. What _____ ? Well, she

   _____ .

7. Mary is looking forward to the holidays. She _____ to the

   seaside.

8. She _____ her holiday there.

b) *Ask Kate, Jenny, etc. about their plans.*

   <u>Example:</u> What are you going to do about your tests?
   Are you going to work harder?

Training 8: The will- or going to-future?

It is Kate's birthday next week. This is what she thinks.

1. If the weather is fine, we _____ play in the garden.

2. I think everybody _____ like that.

3. But I hope Ronny _____ come (not). I _____ to invite him (not).

4. There are still so many things to do. Perhaps Jenny _____ help me.

5. Where is my shopping list? I hope Tom _____ help me with the lemon-

   ade. I _____ ask him when I see him.

6. And who _____ to buy all the rest?

7. What can I do with Timmy? Well, I _____ ask Mum if she can

   take him for a long, long walk. Perhaps he _____ be tired when

   he gets back.

Training 9: Plans for a party

You are planning a party. Say what you are going to do, what will or won't happen, etc. Here are some ideas. Use the going to- or the will-future. Be careful with the tenses.

– ring up my friends
– invite them
– ask them if they can come
– go to a supermarket / buy things
– ask Dad if he can help me / perhaps time to help me
– hope Mum help me, too
– make chips and sausages for us if I ask her
– hope she let us use the dining-room if it rains

 Im Deutschen gebrauchen wir für zukünftige Handlungen meist nicht das Futur, sondern das Präsens. Im Englischen muß dagegen fast immer ein Futur stehen, wenn eine Handlung in der Zukunft stattfindet.

Training 10: With a little help from your friends ...

Translate the following sentences.

1. Morgen schreiben wir einen Englisch-Test.
2. Ich hoffe, er ist nicht zu schwer.
3. Ich hoffe, meine Nachbarin hilft mir.
4. Vielleicht bekomme ich dann eine gute Note.
5. Ich frage sie heute abend, ob sie mir helfen will.
6. Wenn sie mir hilft, gebe ich ihr eine Tafel Schokolade.
7. Ich gebe sie ihr aber nur, wenn ich eine gute Note habe.
8. Wenn ich keine gute Note habe, esse ich die Tafel Schokolade selbst (= myself).

The present perfect

Das present perfect

Die Bildung des present perfect

• Wie du dich sicherlich erinnerst, wird das *present perfect* mit dem Präsens von *have (have/has)* und dem *past participle* (= Partizip der Vergangenheit) gebildet. Die Kurzformen von *have* (='ve/'s) sind natürlich auch möglich.

Tom **hasn't finished** his homework,
but his friends **have** already **arrived.**
Have they **played** with him yet? No, they **haven't.**
They **haven't played** with him yet.

• Verneinte Formen bildest du mit *not*, Fragen durch die Umstellung von Subjekt und *has/have*. Wie bei allen zusammengesetzten Zeiten sind Formen von *to do* bei der Frage und Verneinung nicht möglich. Für die Kurzantworten gelten die üblichen Regeln.

 Bei der Bildung des *past participle* mußt du folgendes beachten:

Infinitiv	*past participle*	regelmäßige Bildung des *past participle*
to finish	he has finish**ed**	finish + ed = finished:
to talk	she has talk**ed**	Das *past participle* bildest du normaler-
to play	they have play**ed**	weise, indem du ein *-ed* an den Infinitiv anhängst.
to arri**v**e	he has arri**ved**	arrive + ed = arrived: Ein auslautendes *-e*, das nicht gespro- chen wird, entfällt.
to sto**p**	he has stop**ped**	stop + ed = stopped: Bei einsilbigen Verben mit kurzem, beton- ten Vokal wird der auslautende Konso- nant verdoppelt.

to cry	he has cr**ied**	cry + ed = cried:
		Nach Konsonant wird y zu *-i*.

Neben den regelmäßigen Formen des *past participle* gibt es – wie im Deutschen – auch unregelmäßige Formen. Diese mußt du auswendig lernen.

Training 1: The past participle

a) *Form the past participle of the following verbs:*

to live	*lived*	to give	
to carry		to play	
to say		to lie	
to show		to feel	
to catch		to think	
to bring		to tell	
to leave		to bet	
to spend		to stand	
to write		to take	

b) *What's the infinitive of these participles?*

paid		taught	
chosen		fallen	
lost		dropped	
thrown		tried	
fed		bought	

Training 2: Holiday plans

The school year isn't over yet, but the Masons are planning their holidays. This year they want to go to the Lake District with their caravan. Have a look at the list and write down what they have already done.

<u>Example:</u> They have already booked a place for July.

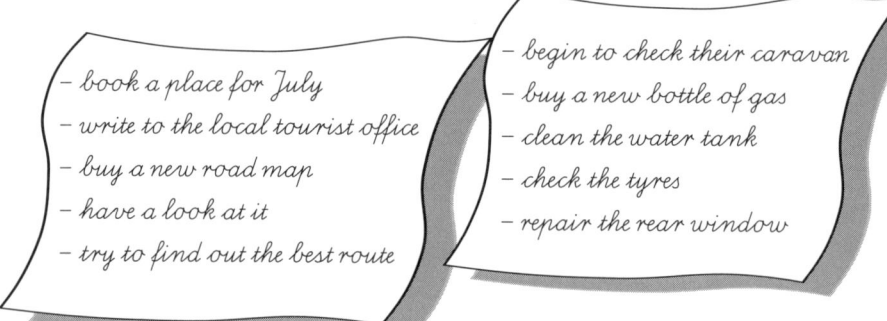

Training 3: Preparations

Two months later, the Masons are at the camping site where they usually have their caravan. They are preparing it for their trip to the Lake District. Mr and Mrs Mason have made a list of the things they have to do.

When they get home, Mrs Mason has a look at the list. She says to her husband: *"Look, there are still some things to do. We have washed the caravan, but we haven't cleaned the floor yet."* Go on.

Training 4: Timmy's questions

Timmy is very excited. He wants to know what has happened to his things. Ask his questions. Example: Have you seen my potty?

– put my telephone in the caravan   – take away my pencils

– buy a new picture book for   – put it in the caravan

     – buy some chocolate   – pack my swimming things

– see my teddy   – find my red toy car

Training 5: A last check

Before they leave, Mr Mason asks everybody :

Mrs Mason: Yes, *we have* _____ .

"Let me see … Have we shut

all the windows?"

"Have you turned off the gas, Tom?"

Tom: Yes, _____ .

"Have you locked the back door, Kate?"

Kate: Yes, _____ .

"Have you all been to the toilet?"

All: Yes, _____ .

"Have you switched off the lights in

your room?"

Tom: Yes, _____ .

"Has Timmy had something to drink?"

Tom: Yes, _____ .

"Have you lost your teddy again, Timmy?"

"Have we forgotten anything?"

Timmy: No, _____ .

"Can we go now?"

All: No, _____ .

Timmy: "No, we _____ .

I've left my teddy upstairs."

Die Wortstellung beim present perfect

Have	you	washed	**your hands?**
Hv	S	Vb	Objekt

		Objekt	Vb
Hast	du	**deine Hände**	gewaschen?

Wie bei anderen zusammengesetzten Zeiten steht das Objekt im Englischen immer hinter der Verbgruppe. Von den Signalwörtern, die häufig mit dem *present perfect* gebraucht werden, stehen:

never	(niemals)	unmittelbar
ever	(jemals)	vor dem Verb
already	(schon)	
yet	(schon)	am Satzende
not ... yet	(noch nicht)	

Have you **already** packed your things?   I have**n't** packed my clothes **yet.**
Have you **ever** been late?   Have you finished **yet**?
I have **never** been late.

Training 6: Questions and answers

Ask six questions and answer them.

Have	your brother		have	
Have	you	ever	be	to a caravan site?
Has	your father	already	clean	a caravan?
	your sister	never	work	to England?
	your friends		go	on a caravan holiday?
			have	an accident?
			drive	a caravan?
			sleep	in a caravan?
			push	lunch in a caravan?
			play	

Example: Have you ever driven a caravan? – No, I haven't. I've never driven a caravan.

          or: – No, I haven't driven a caravan yet.

Training 7: Let's put it right

Put the following sentences in their correct order.

1. everything   the Masons   packed   have   already

---

2. They   in the caravan   all their things   have   put

---

3. They   already   done   100 kilometres   have

---

4. But they   not   arrived   have   yet   at their camping-site

---

5. not   yet   been   Timmy   sick   has

---

6. He is hungry now. He   not yet   has   breakfast   yet   had

---

7. But he   already   been   on his potty   four times   has

---

to be sick - sich übergeben

Der Gebrauch des present perfect

"We **have washed** the caravan. It's clean now."
"Where are my car keys? I hope I **haven't lost** them."
"**Have you seen** them? Do you know where they are?"

Das *present perfect* gebraucht man für Handlungen, die zwar vorbei sind,
die aber ein Ergebnis haben, das in der Gegenwart noch wirksam ist.

Training 8: Results

What are the results? Complete the second sentence.

Example: The Masons have washed their caravan. It's clean now.

1. I have listened to you. I know what you _____

2. I have done my homework. Here _____

3. I have made my teacher angry. He _____

4. I have read this book. I _____

5. I haven't seen this film. I _____

6. I haven't cleaned my room yet. It _____

Training 9: What has happened?

Can you finish these sentences?

There's lipstick
on Tom's face.
(Jenny – kiss him
goodbye)

Here are Mr Mason's
car keys.
(find again)

Here is Timmy's potty.
(Timmy – put it in the
fridge)

Here are the Masons
in front of their cara-
van. They are ready to
leave. (pack everything)

Look at that window.
It's not shut.
(somebody forget to
shut it)

That's the street where the
Masons live. It's empty now.
(The Masons – leave)

Example: There's lipstick on Tom's face. Jenny has kissed him goodbye.

The simple past

Das simple past

Die Bildung des simple past

The children are back at school. They are talking about the things that they did in their holidays:

Mike:
> We **visited** the Isle of Wight and **did** quite a lot of things there. I even **tried** to talk to some Germans there, but they just **laughed** when I **tried** to say something in German to them. I think my German **sounded** a bit funny to them. So I **stopped** speaking German to them and **laughed** at their English.

Tom:
> We **went** to the Lake District. We **found** a fantastic camping site and **had** a great time there. Only Timmy **had** a bad time. One day he … but I'll tell you about that later.

Jenny:
> I **was** in London. I **stayed** there with my aunt and my uncle. They **were** very strict and never **let** me go out alone. It's too dangerous for girls like you, they **said.**

 Bei den regelmäßigen Formen wird das *simple past* wie das *past participle* mit dem Infinitiv + *ed* gebildet. Beachte dabei die folgenden Regeln:

1. Bei Verben, die auf ein nicht gesprochenes -*e* enden, fällt ein *e* aus:
   cycl**e** + **ed**   = cycl**ed**

2. Nach Konsonant + *y* wird das *y* zu *i*. Nach Vokal bleibt das *y* erhalten (vgl. auch die Pluralbildung und die 3. Person Sg. im *simple present*).

try + **ed** = tr**ied**
sta**y** + **ed** = st**ayed**

3. Einsilbige Verben mit kurzem, betontem Vokal, die auf Konsonant enden, verdoppeln den letzten Konsonant:

sto**p** + **ed** = sto**pped**

Unregelmäßige Formen

Wie im Deutschen gibt es auch im Englischen unregelmäßige Formen, die du einfach lernen mußt. Einige findest du oben im Text.

Die Formen des *simple past* sind für alle Personen gleich. Dies gilt sowohl für die regelmäßigen wie die unregelmäßigen Formen. Im übrigen: Ein *-s* in der dritten Person Singular gibt es nur im *simple present* und bei den Formen von *to be*.

Das simple past von to be

Auch die Formen von *to be* sind unregelmäßig. Sie lauten:

I	**was**	we	**were**
you	**were**	you	**were**
he, she, it	**was**	they	**were**

Training 1: Mind the spelling and the pronunciation

Mark the regular and irregular verbs with different colours.

say   stop   lead   read
    buy   write
play   sit   tear
   cry   catch   set   ride
carry   swim   hear
    think   feed   hide
fly   let   meet   break
   bring   lose   get   hit
      teach

Training 2: The Masons leave

Put in the missing verbs. Use the simple past.

> know   want   arrive   be   leave   carry   see
>
> come   go   see   run   hear   shut   get

The Masons _____ to leave early, but as usual it _____ quite late

when they _____ off. Kate _____ still tired and Tom _____

to finish a letter. Then Timmy's potty _____ missing and nobody

_____ where it _____ . When they _____ all in the car again,

somebody _____ that a window _____ still open. So Mr Mason

_____ out of the car, _____ into the house again and

_____ it. When he _____ back, Timmy _____ to go to the

toilet again. So Mr Mason _____ out of the car again and _____

Timmy to the bathroom. When they_____ back, they _____ the

telephone ringing. So Tom _____ out of the car and _____ into the

house again. But he _____ not fast enough. When he _____ , the

line _____ dead. But finally they _____ ready to leave.

Training 3: The Masons' trip

Retell the Masons' trip to their camping site. Use the simple past.

finally leave at 11 o'clock	first stop at 11.30/ Timmy sick*	second stop at 12.15/Timmy sick again	lunch at 1 p.m./ when leave/forget Timmy's teddy
get in car at 2 p.m./drive on	Mr Mason take a short cut/ lose two hours	arrive at 6 p.m. at the camping site/try to put up tent* for Tom/tent collapse*	have supper at 8/ go to bed at 9/ all very tired

* to be sick – sich übergeben   a tent – Zelt   to collapse – zusammenbrechen

Verneinte Formen

Timmy	**did not** (= **didn't**)	enjoy	the trip.
He	**did not** (= **didn't**)	feel	fine.

| Subjekt | + | did not (= didn't) + | Infinitiv |

Timmy	**was not** (= **wasn't**)	happy.
Tom and Kate	**were not** (= **weren't**)	sick.

| Subjekt | + | was/were not |

- Vollverben werden im *simple past* mit *did not* bzw. *didn't* verneint. Danach steht immer der Infinitiv.
- *Was/were* werden mit *not* verneint. Statt *was not/were not* sind auch die entsprechenden Kurzformen *(wasn't/weren't)* möglich.

Training 4: The first night

Write out these sentences. Use negative forms.

The first night Timmy not sleep very well – not have his teddy – not quiet enough at the camping site – at home not sleep in the same bed with Kate – his sister not leave him enough room – she not want him in "her" bed – Timmy not warm enough – not have nice dreams – not happy that night.

Training 5: The first day

Write down what they did the first day.

Example: The first day they didn't get up early. They had a late breakfast.

Timmy Tom Kate Mr Mason Mrs Mason	not cook in the caravan not sick any more not do any work not get up early not do any homework not lie on the beach not stay in the caravan not feel tired any more	write a letter to Jenny. have a late breakfast go for a walk buy a new teddy for Timmy have lunch in a restaurant look for new friends feel better walk around the camping site

Fragen und Kurzantworten

Did	you have a nice holiday?		Yes, I **did.**
Didn't	you go swimming?		No, I **didn't.**

Wenn du eine Frage im *simple past* mit Vollverben bilden willst, muß du *did* bzw. *didn't* gebrauchen. Danach steht immer ein Infinitiv. In Kurzantworten wird das Vollverb durch *did* bzw. *didn't* ersetzt.

Were	you	on the beach?	No, I **wasn't.**
Was	the water	cold?	Yes, it **was.**
Weren't	you	unhappy?	No, I **wasn't.**

Bei *to be* darfst du keine Form von *to do* gebrauchen. Du bildest die Frage allein durch Umstellung von Subjekt und Prädikat. Bei Kurzantworten stehen die entsprechenden Formen von *to be*.

Training 6: Questions

When Tom was back from his holidays, his friends asked him a lot of questions. Complete the questions and give short answers.

1. _____ go to the Lake District for the first time? (Yes)

2. _____ you like it there? (Yes)

3. _____ you sleep in a tent? (Yes)

4. _____ it cold at night? (No)

5. _____ you go swimming? (Yes)

6. _____ you make any friends? (Yes)

7. _____ there any other girls? (Yes)

8. _____ you like them? (No)

9. _____ they nicer than Jenny? (No)

10. _____ they older than you? (Yes)

Fragen mit Fragewörtern

a) nach dem Subjekt   b) nach allen anderen Satzteilen

Who	was on the beach?	Where	was	Timmy?	
What	happened?	What	did	he	do there?
Who	didn't come back?	Why	didn't	he	come back?
Who	broke his arm?	What	did	he	break?

Auch bei Ergänzungsfragen, d. h. Fragen mit Fragewörtern, mußt du *did* oder
didn't gebrauchen. Bei Fragen nach dem Subjekt ist *didn't* dagegen nur in
verneinten Fragen möglich. Bei Fragen mit *to be* steht dagegen nie ein *did*!

Training 7: Tom's letter

> Dear Mike,
> Something terrible happened yesterday. I wanted to go to
> the beach with Timmy and Kate. Timmy had his teddy and
> his picture book in his hands, so perhaps he didn't see
> where he was going. Anyway - suddenly Timmy stumbled*
> and fell over a big stone. I turned round and saw that it
> was Timmy. He still had his teddy in his right hand; but
> his arm looked strange. Timmy didn't cry at first, but his
> face looked very white. I didn't know what to do, so I told
> Kate to run home and to fetch Mum or Dad. Kate did
> what I told her and five minutes later Mum and Dad
> were there. They carried Timmy back to the caravan and
> phoned a doctor. When she came, she examined Timmy ...

*When Mr and Mrs Mason saw Kate, they knew that something had happened.
Imagine what they asked Kate.*

* to stumble – stolpern

Training 8: At the hospital

Well, Timmy had to go to hospital. A doctor examined him again. Ask the doctor's questions. Here are some ideas to help you.

Example: Did it hurt, Timmy?

– hurt?	– fall on your arm?	– your teddy all right?
– how?	– cry?	– who help you?
– why?	– when?	– anybody with you?

Die Vergangenheit von einigen Hilfsverben

When the doctor examined Timmy, he found out that Timmy's arm was broken.

So Timmy **couldn't** go home.
His parents **couldn't** take him home.
But they **could** come and talk to him.

His parents **were allowed to** visit him.
He **was not allowed to** get up the first day.
But he **was allowed to** get up the next day.

He **had to** stay in hospital for some days.
Did he **have to** stay in bed all the time? No, he didn't.
He **didn't have to** stay in bed all the time.

Von den englischen Hilfsverben hat nur *can* (= können) eine Vergangenheitsform (*could/could not* bzw. die Kurzform *couldn't* = konnte/konnte nicht). Für die anderen Hilfsverben mußt du Ersatzverben (= sogenannte *substitutes*) verwenden und zwar für:

may	(dürfen)	was/were allowed to	(durfte)
may not/mustn't	(nicht dürfen)	wasn't/weren't allowed to	(durfte nicht)
must	(müssen)	had to	(mußte)
needn't	(nicht müssen/ nicht brauchen)	didn't have to	(mußte nicht/ brauchte nicht)

Nach Hilfsverben und Ersatzverben steht immer ein Infinitiv. Bei Hilfsverben steht jedoch – im Unterschied zu Ersatzverben – kein *to* vor dem Infinitiv.

Training 9: At the hospital

The first day after his operation there were some things Timmy was not allowed to do or couldn't do. What could he do? What was he allowed to do? What did he have to do?

– play with his teddy

– draw pictures with his right arm   – talk to the nurses

– run around in the room

– make his bed

– look at his picture book   – be careful with his arm

– keep his arm still (= ruhig)

– clean the room   – play in the corridor

– stay in bed all day

– eat his meals

Training 10: Questions

Now ask Timmy what he had to do and what he was allowed to do.

Example: Did you have to stay in bed all the time? – No, I didn't.

Training 11: Prescriptions

Complete the text. Use substitutes.

After three days the Masons *were allowed* to take Timmy home. They

_____ to leave the camping site and break off their holidays, the doc-

tors told them, but there were some things that Timmy _____ to do. He

_____ to stay in the caravan all day, but he _____ to be very

careful with his arm. He _____ to play any wild games and above all,

he _____ to swim. He _____ to take any medicine, and they

_____ to worry, but they _____ to see that Timmy didn't fall

down again.

The simple past and the
past progressive

Kapitel 16

Das simple past und das
past progressive im Vergleich

Der Gebrauch des simple past

Mr Mason **had** an accident, too.
But it **was** many years ago.
When **did** he have the accident?
It **was** in 1975, when he **was** much
younger than today.

1. Das *simple past* steht bei Handlungen, die in der Vergangenheit
stattfanden und abgeschlossen
sind. Es findet sich nach Signalwörtern wie *yesterday, a (week, a
month, year) ago, last (Friday,
month), in 1995*. Oft steht es auch
nach *when*.

He **played** in a football team then.
They **played** every Saturday.
His team **wasn't** a good team, so
they often **lost.**
But sometimes they also **won.**

2. bei wiederholten und gewohn-
heitsmäßigen Handlungen, die in
der Vergangenheit stattfanden.
Signalwörter sind hier – wie
schon beim *simple present* –
always, usually, often, sometimes,
etc.

He remembered one match:
They **were** on their way home when
their bus suddenly **ran** off the road.
He **felt** a pain in his left leg, and
things **went** black before his eyes.
Then he **didn't feel** anything else.
Afterwards, they **told** him that his left
leg was broken.

3. das *simple past* wird verwendet
für abgeschlossene, aufeinanderfolgende Handlungen der Vergangenheit. Signalwörter sind hier
*first, then, after that, the next mo-
ment, the next morning, last night,
when, suddenly,* etc.

Training 1: What happened after the accident?

Tell Timmy's story. Use first, then, after that, so, when, etc. to connect the sentences.

Tom send Kate back to parents	Kate run to caravan	Kate tell parents all about Timmy's accident	Mrs Mason phone a doctor
doctor arrive/ examine Timmy	call an ambulance	ambulance arrive/ the ambulance men put Timmy on a stretcher*	drive him to the hospital

* stretcher – Bahre

Das past progressive

What **were** the Masons **doing** when Timmy had his accident?
Were they **going** to the beach, too? No, they **weren't.**

Mr Mason **was talking** to a neighbour.
They **were having** a coke and talking about football.
Mrs Mason **was reading** a book.
She **wasn't listening** to what they **were talking** about.

- Das *past progressive* wird mit *was/were* und dem *present participle* gebildet. Bei Fragen wird umgestellt (Hilfsverb – Subjekt – Verb); verneinte Formen werden mit *not* gebildet. *To do* ist bei Fragen und bei der Verneinung nicht möglich. Zur Bildung des *present participle* vergleiche Kapitel 8.

Nicht alle Verben können im Englischen eine *progressive form* bilden. Verben wie *to be, to belong, to see, to feel, to hear, to want, to like, to know, to think, to sound* u. a. haben im Englischen meist keine *progressive form*. Hier mußt du die *simple forms* gebrauchen.

Training 2: What people were doing

When Timmy had his accident, a lot of people were on the beach. Say what they were doing.

- a woman reading a magazine
- a man lying in a deckchair
- some people swimming
- two children playing with a ball

- a girl putting on her clothes
- a boy listening to a radio
- a family having a picnic

Training 3: Asking people

You are the reporter of the local newspaper. You want to find out what people were doing when Timmy had his accident. So you ask them.

Example: What were you doing when the accident happened?
Were you having a swim?

Go on.

The simple past und das past progressive

Neu einsetzende oder neue Handlungen: *simple past*

Gleichzeitigkeit mit neuer Handlung: *past progressive*

When the ambulance arrived,

Timmy was still lying on the beach. He was crying. A lot of people were standing around him.

Was geschah dann? (neue Handlung)

The ambulance men examined Timmy. Then they put him on a stretcher and drove him off to hospital.

Und dann? (neue Handlung)

Was passierte gerade zu dieser Zeit?

When the ambulance left,

the people were still standing there.

- Wie du bereits weißt, steht das *simple past* für Handlungen, die vorüber sind und einander folgen. Solche Handlungsketten kommen vor allem in Erzählungen und Berichten vor. Hier liegt auch der Grund dafür, warum du das *simple past* in einer Geschichte oder einem Bericht für jede neu einsetzende Handlung verwenden mußt.

- Im Unterschied zum *simple past* mußt du das *past progressive* für Handlungen verwenden, die zu dem Zeitpunkt noch nicht vorüber waren, als eine neue Handlung eintrat. Handlungen im *past progressive* bilden daher sozusagen den Hintergrund für neu einsetzende Handlungen. Ein häufiges Signalwort für eine solche Hintergrundshandlung ist hier *while*.

- Im Deutschen steht für das *past progressive* oft „gerade". Vergleiche:
  Tom **was talking** to Kate when Timmy **fell over**.
  (… redete gerade)

Training 4: Your idea

The Masons had one neighbour who didn't like them. So he told people a lot of bad things about them.

| When poor Timmy broke his arm, | Mr Mason his wife nobody Kate Tom | just get up drink beer with their neighbours look after Timmy lie in the sun smoke and talk still lie in bed write a letter just have breakfast |

Write six sentences.

Training 5: At the hospital

Tell the story. Use the correct tenses.

1. While they (sit) in the waiting-room/ the door (open). A man (come) in.

2. He (wear) a bandage round his head.

3. He (say) good morning/then he (sit) down/(look) for a newspaper.

4. He (open) newspaper/ (begin) to read.

5. While (read) his newspaper, a nurse (come) in.

6. She (tell) Mr Mason and Mrs Mason to follow her.

7. She (lead) them to the room where Timmy (wait).

8. There a doctor (talk) to Timmy.

9. Timmy (ask) him a lot of questions.

10. When the doctor (see) them/(call) them to Timmy's bed.

11. Timmy (laugh). He (be) happy he (can) go home.

12. They (thank) the doctor/(pack) Timmy's things. Then they (leave) the hospital.

Training 6: In the waiting-room

A few days later, the Masons were allowed to take Timmy home. But they had to wait until Timmy was ready. There were a lot of patients in the waiting-room who had to wait for the doctor, too. Why were they waiting for the doctor?

play football/
fall to the ground/
broke my arm* rib – Rippe

climb a rock/
slip

I slip/have a shower/
broke three ribs*

*   rib – Rippe

I clean the windows/
ladder break/
fall onto the floor

I lie in my deckchair/
it collapse

I do my homework/
fall asleep/
fall off the chair

Training 7: A ghost story

The simple past or the past progressive?

Timmy still _____ (have) to be very careful with his arm and he

_____ (can't) go for a swim, of course. So everybody _____ (have)

to keep him busy. Tom often _____ (read) ghost stories to him. Timmy's

favourite story _____ (be) about an American family who _____

(want) to buy an old castle in England. When they _____ (come) to the

castle, the sun _____ (not shine). It _____ (rain) and thunder

_____ (sound) again and again. When they _____ (enter) the

castle, a flash of lightning* _____ (fill) the hall and there _____ (be)

lightning and thunder all through the night. The next morning when they

_____ (come) down, they _____ (see) blood* on the floor. The next

night they _____ (hear) strange noises in the corridor outside their bed-

rooms. When Mr Otis _____ (open) the door, he _____ (see) a ter-

rible old man. Long hair _____ (fall) from his head, his eyes _____

(be) like fire and he...

* lightning – Blitz
* blood – Blut

The simple past and
the present perfect

Das simple past und das present perfect im Vergleich

Zum Gebrauch des present perfect und des simple past

present perfect

für Handlungen, die zwar vorbei sind, aber in der Gegenwart noch Folgen haben:

The Masons **have packed** everything.
They **have turned off** the gas.
They **have** already **locked** the door.
They **have paid for** the camping site, too.

Das *present perfect* betont das gegenwärtige Ergebnis. Es steht daher meist ohne eine Zeitangabe der Vergangenheit. Mit dem *present perfect* gebrauchte Signalwörter sind: *already, yet, not ... yet, never, ever,* etc.

simple past

für Handlungen, die abgeschlossen und daher vorüber sind:

They **packed** yesterday.
They **turned** the gas **off** after breakfast.
When **did** they **lock** the door?
They **paid** ten weeks ago.

Das *simple past* betont, daß Handlungen vorbei sind. Es steht daher oft mit Zeitangaben der Vergangenheit wie *ago, yesterday, at that time, last week, in 1983*; häufig auch bei *when*.

Bei allen diesen Zeitangaben der Vergangenheit muß unbedingt das *simple past* stehen!

Training 1: Back at school

All the children are back at school. They ask each other lots of questions. Complete these questions. Put in the simple past or the present perfect.

1. When _____ you _____ (come) back?

2. Where _____ you _____ (go?)

3. _____ you _____ (like) your stay there?

4. _____ ever _____ (be) to Italy?

5. _____ you _____ (do) anything for school as Old Misery

_____ (tell) you?

6. _____ you _____ (play) tennis in the holidays?

7. How many postcards _____ you _____ (write)?

8. Where _____ you _____ (buy) these shoes?

9. What _____ (be) the weather like? _____ it _____ (rain) a lot?

10. _____ you already_____ (see) Mike? Is he late again?

Training 2: Your answers

Can you answer the questions in Training 2?

Training 3: Mike's photos

During the holidays Mike took a lot of photos. He is showing them to Tom and Jenny. Complete the sentences and put in the correct tenses (simple present, simple past, present perfect).

Look! This our hotel/stay there for two weeks

That is the beach in front of our hotel/always go swimming there

This is our car/ accident/we not repair it yet

This is Carisbrooke Castle/visit the castle/you know that Charles I prisoner here?

That is Tim/I play with him a lot/we often go to the beach/have a swim together

And that girl is his sister/we play with her sometimes

Training 4: Mike's "new life"

Mike's last school report wasn't very good, so during the holidays he made plans to begin a "new life". He made a list of the things he wanted to do. After three weeks at school he had a look at the list again and added two or three things to it. Then he read it to himself.

<u>Example:</u> I haven't been late any more. I was only late the first day.

  Go on.

be late any more (only the first day)

listen to my teachers (nearly always!)

not play during lessons (never again)

talk to my neighbour (only sometimes)

not forget my books again (only yesterday)

do my homework in all subjects (only not do it last Monday)

go home immediately after school (usually)

write better tests (got good marks!)

learn more German (spend nearly ten minutes on my German homework yesterday!)

not watch so much TV (yesterday only one hour!)

Der deutsche und englische Gebrauch des present perfect

Das Perfekt im Deutschen
„… gestern **sind** wir **heimgekommen; wir haben** unser Gepäck aus dem Auto **geholt** und **haben** dann zu Abend **gegessen.** Dann **sind** wir ins Bett **gegangen** und **sind** sofort **eingeschlafen.**"

Das *simple past* im Englischen
"… yesterday we **came** home; we **fetched** our luggage from the car; then we **had** supper. After that we **went** to bed and **fell** asleep immediately."

In der deutschen Umgangssprache gebraucht man das Perfekt vor allem dazu, eine Geschichte zu erzählen oder über etwas zu berichten. Dies ist im Englischen nicht möglich.

Wenn man im Englischen etwas erzählen oder berichten will, gebraucht man das *simple past*. Es ist die eigentliche Erzählzeit im Englischen und findet sich vor allem nach Signalwörtern wie *first, then, after that, at that moment, suddenly* etc.

Training 5: The first lesson

As you know, Tom and his class have German, too. In the first lesson after the holidays they had to tell old Old Misery, their German teacher, about their holidays. They had to do it in German. This is what they told him. Can you put in English what they said?

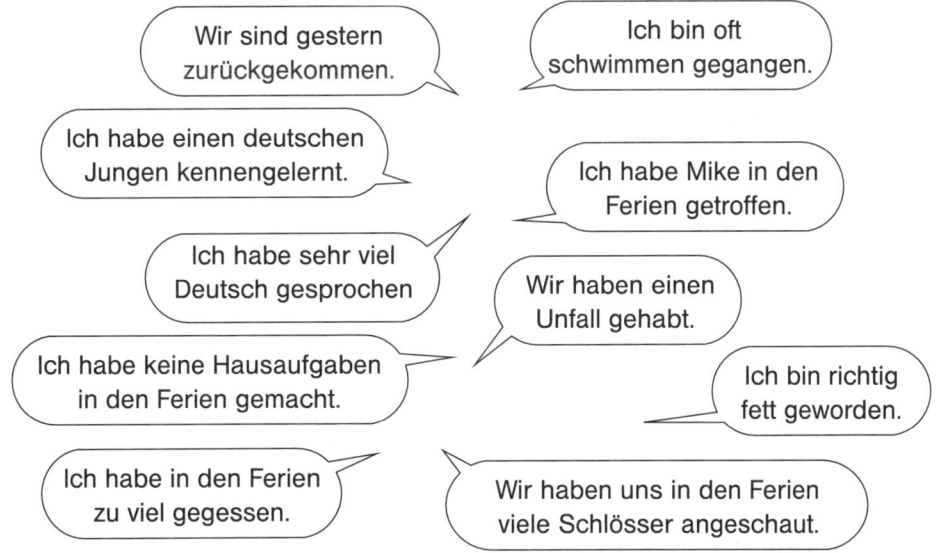

Wir sind gestern zurückgekommen.

Ich bin oft schwimmen gegangen.

Ich habe einen deutschen Jungen kennengelernt.

Ich habe Mike in den Ferien getroffen.

Ich habe sehr viel Deutsch gesprochen

Wir haben einen Unfall gehabt.

Ich habe keine Hausaufgaben in den Ferien gemacht.

Ich bin richtig fett geworden.

Ich habe in den Ferien zu viel gegessen.

Wir haben uns in den Ferien viele Schlösser angeschaut.

Training 6: A ghost story

In one of the first lessons Tom's class had to write about a holiday adventure. These are Mike's notes for his story. Can you write it out? Be careful with the tenses.

In the holidays we visit Carisbrooke Castle – old castle – famous, too, because Charles I prisoner there some hundred years ago, before his execution. People say – he not found peace yet – his ghost still walk there.

When we get there, the sky very dark – when walk through the entrance – begin to rain – so go into the castle – very dark in there, too; lots of strange noises suddenly a door open – when I look there – I see something green – come towards me – run out of the building and tell everything to my parents – not believe me – just laugh at me.

Two days after the holidays over – we must go home again – That night I go to bed early, but wake up at midnight – strange noise – see something green – it sit at my desk – before I can say anything, it gone – soon forget this, but two weeks later I wake up again – see a green shadow at my desk again – it write something in an exercise book – I very afraid, not move – five minutes later it gone. As it not come back, I get up – go to the desk – there see my German exercise book – open – a note in the book: Don't do any homework tomorrow or you'll die! This is what the ghost tell me – that's why I not do any homework last Tuesday.

Training 7: So sorry, but …

Not all pupils like homework. Here is a list of things you can say when you have forgotten it. Use the correct tenses.

		my neighbour (be) ill.
		I (not remember) where I (put) it.
		I (leave) my book at school.
	B	I (leave) it on the bus/at home.
	E	my mother father/sister (be) ill yesterday.
I couldn't do my homework	C	I (feel) so ill in the afternoon.
I can't show you my homework	A	my pen (not work).
	U	I (forget) my schoolbag.
	S	my baby brother/baby sister (eat) it.
	E	my exercise book (be) full.
		my baby brother (make) a plane out of it.
		I (must) repair my bike.
		my mother (not have) time to do it.

Adjectives

Kapitel 18

Adjektive

Der Gebrauch der Adjektive

What do you think? Are there any **nice** and **clever** girls/boys in your class?
Or are they all **silly** and **stupid**?

Adjektive beziehen sich immer auf Substantive oder Pronomen. Dabei geben
sie Eigenschaften der jeweiligen Sachen oder Personen an.

Wie im Deutschen steht das Adjektiv meist unmittelbar vor dem Substantiv
(a nice boy); nach bestimmten Verben wie to be steht es auch nach dem
Substantiv:

Tom **is nice.**

Training 1: What's your English teacher, friend, brother, sister like?

Choose three adjectives for each person.

Example: What's your English teacher like?
Let me see – she is clever and intelligent, but she can be strange, too.

bad
beautiful
good
boring   busy   careful
crazy

exciting
fantastic
noisy
fat   loud
modern
poor

powerful
quick
slow
strange   tall
small
thin

strong
worried   clever
intelligent
funny
heavy

dangerous
interesting
nice
wonderful   difficult

Training 2: What you think

Choose at least three adjectives from the list in Training 1 to show what you think about

English tests   **boys**   **teachers**

   comics   **TV**

      books

                  baby brothers/sisters

         films

  pop music   **football**

            girls

Example: Girls are nice, clever and intelligent.

Training 3: What's the opposite?

Example: A good teacher – a bad teacher

a funny girl   _____   a clever pupil   _____

an old town   _____   a quiet boy   _____

a small boy   _____   a happy child   _____

a good mark   _____   a difficult text   _____

a boring film   _____   a silly person   _____

a fast runner   _____   a terrible story   _____

a bad driver   _____   a rich man   _____

Die Steigerung der Adjektive

Adjektive werden im Englischen wie folgt gesteigert:

	Positiv	Komparativ	Superlativ
einsilbige Adjektive	poor	poor**er**	the poor**est**
	fine	fin**er**	the fin**est**
	big	big**ger**	the big**gest**

zweisilbige Adjektive	funny	funn**ier**	the funn**iest**
auf -y und -er	angry	angr**ier**	the angr**iest**
	clever	clever**er**	the clever**est**

die meisten anderen	famous	**more** famous	the **most** famous
zweisilbigen Adjektive	terrible	**more** terrible	the **most** terrible
sowie alle Adjektive mit	difficult	**more** difficult	the **most** difficult
drei und mehr Silben			

1. Adjektive mit einer Silbe und zweisilbige Adjektive auf -y und -er bilden den Komparativ mit -er und den Superlativ mit -est. Dabei entfällt ein auslautendes -e.
2. Einsilbige Adjektive mit einem kurzen, betonten Vokal, die auf Konsonant enden, verdoppeln den auslautenden Konsonanten.
3. Zweisilbige Adjektive, die nicht auf -y und -er enden, sowie alle Adjektive, die mehr als zwei Silben haben, bilden den Komparativ mit *more* und den Superlativ mit *most*.

Die folgenden Adjektive haben unregelmäßige Steigerungsformen:

| good | better | the best |
| bad | worse | the worst |

Der Vergleich im Satz

Die verschiedenen Formen der Adjektive benutzt man dazu, Vergleiche zu ziehen. Gleichheit bzw. Ungleichheit werden folgendermaßen ausgedrückt:

Gleichheit:

| Mike is **as** tall **as** Tom. | ... (eben)so ... wie ...**as** + Positiv + **as** |
| Is he also **as** intelligent? | ... (eben)so ... |

Ungleichheit:

Tom's sister **isn't as** tall **as** Mike.	... nicht so ... wie...	not **as** + Pos. + **as**
She is smaller **than** Mike.	... kleiner als ...	Komparativ + **than**
But she is **more** intelligent **than** Mike.	... intelligenter als ...	

Vor und nach der Grundform des Adjektivs steht immer *as*, nach dem Komparativ dagegen immer *than*.
Verwechsle *than* (= als) nicht mit *then* (= dann, damals).

Training 4: Comparatives and superlatives

Form the comparatives and superlatives of the following adjectives:

good, careful, noisy, fat, powerful, nice, intelligent, heavy, dangerous, quick

Training 5: Tom's family

Compare the persons in the picture. Use the superlatives and comparatives of tall and small.

Dad 1.85 cm	Mum 1.70 cm	Grandfather 1.80 cm	Grandmother 1.65 cm
Tom 1.52 cm	Kate 1.40 cm	Timmy 0.92 cm	

Training 6: Comparisons

Susan and Betty, two girls in Tom's class, don't like each other. So their ideas are often different.

<u>Example:</u> Susan: I think football is more exciting than volleyball.
Betty: No, it isn't, but it's more dangerous.
Susan: More dangerous? I think volleyball is as dangerous as football.

tennis	difficult	English	nice	comics	funny
swimming	expensive	German	useful	books	interesting

Training 7: What girls whisper

Susan and Jane are talking about Mike, the new boy in class. Can you complete what they say?
Use the following adjectives: tall, strong, silly, bad, good, nice in their different forms.

Susan: He is very tall. I think he is _____ boy in our class.

Jane: Is he? No, I think David is _____ him.

Susan: And he's so strong. He must be _____ boy in our class.

Jane: He is very nice. I think he is even _____ than Tom.

Susan: Look at his hair. It has got the same colour _____ your hair. Have you got the same shoes, too?

Jane: Oh, don't be stupid; or you'll get a prize for _____ questions.

Susan: Is he good at maths? Do you think he can help me? I need somebody who is _____ Tom. You know, at maths Tom is even _____ me.

Jane: Why don't you go and ask him? He looks a bit silly, but perhaps he is _____ at maths _____ he looks.

Susan: Have you seen any of his photos? Anne told me his photos are _____ photos she has ever seen.

Training 8: Questions – questions

You have almost finished this book now. Can you answer some questions?

1. Has your English become _____ (good)?

2. Let's hope it hasn't become _____ (bad).

3. Is the number of mistakes in your English tests _____ or _____

   (big/small) now?

4. Were the exercises very _____ (boring)?

5. Were they _____ (interesting) than in your textbook?

6. Were they _____ (boring) as in your textbook?

7. Or were they _____ (bad)?

8. Was the grammar _____ (clear) enough?

9. Or was the grammar in your textbook _____ (easy)?

10. We hope that you didn't find things too _____ (difficult).

English word order

Die Wortstellung im Englischen

Die Stellung des Subjekts im Aussagesatz

Da englische Substantive außer der Pluralendung keine Endungen haben, liegt die Wortstellung im Englischen fest. Du kannst daher die Wortstellung nicht einfach ändern, ohne daß sich auch der Sinn des Satzes ändert. Vergleiche:

The dog	bites	the postman.	Der Hund beißt den Briefträger (= Objekt).
The postman	bites	the dog.	Der Briefträger (= Subjekt) beißt den Hund.

Wie du aus diesem Beispiel siehst, bestimmt im Englischen die Wortstellung die Funktion eines Substantivs (oder Pronomens): Steht es in einem Aussagesatz vor dem Verb, ist es Subjekt. Steht es nach dem Verb, ist es Objekt des Aussagesatzes. Aus diesem Grunde sind auch andere Umstellungen, die du vom Deutschen her kennst, im Englischen nicht möglich:

Heute	habe	ich Kopfweh.		Today	I	have got a headache.
Heute	bin	ich krank.		Today	I	am ill.
	Verb	Subjekt		*Zeit*	Subj.	Verb

 Im englischen Aussagesatz steht das Subjekt immer vor dem Verb. Es wird auch dann nicht umgestellt, wenn ihm ein anderer Satzteil vorausgeht.

Training 1: What you can do or say

Write as many sentences as you can. Begin with the subordinate clause.

Example: Before I go to school, I usually do my homework.

What do you	say do think	before you go to school? when you don't want to go to school? when it's too cold to get up? when you are late? when you must do your homework? when you must go to bed? before you get up? before you have breakfast? when you go to bed? when you can't find your homework?

Training 2: A week in Jenny's life

Jenny always takes down in a calendar what she wants to do. This is a week in her life. Ask Jenny what she is going to do.

Example: What are you going to do on Monday, Jenny? Well, let me see …
          On Monday, I …

Monday:	4 p.m. table tennis with Tom
Tuesday:	8.15 p.m. watch film on TV
Wednesday:	after school learn for German test with Tom
Thursday:	6 p.m. help Kate with maths homework
Friday:	5 p.m. buy birthday present for Sarah/ring up Sarah
Saturday:	Sarah's birthday party at 2 p.m.
Sunday:	ring up Tom/go for a walk with Tom at 4 p.m.

Training 3: Your plans

What are your plans for the next week? What are you going to do on Monday, Tuesday, etc?

Example: On Monday, I'm going to play football.
          On Tuesday, …

          Go on.

Training 4: Tom's homework

For his German homework, Tom must write eight sentences in German. Here they are. Can you put them into English?

Homework
1. Heute bin ich krank.
2. Heute muß ich nicht aufstehen.
3. Heute kann ich im Bett bleiben.
4. Heute muß ich nicht in die Schule gehen.
5. Heute muß ich keine Hausaufgaben machen.
6. Heute habe ich kein Deutsch.
7. Heute habe ich Fieber.
8. Heute ist ein schöner Tag.

Die Stellung der Objekte

Subjekt	Verb	Objekt
Tom	has got	a sister.
He	likes	her.
He	is buying	her an ice cream.
She	likes	ice cream.
He	must buy	an ice cream for Timmy, too.

Objekte stehen im Englischen immer nach dem Verb oder der Verbgruppe. Im Englischen dürfen keine Satzteile zwischen dem Verb und dem Objekt stehen.

Training 5: At the school cafeteria

Not all the pupils like what they can eat at the school cafeteria. Mike, for example, doesn't like beans. What about the others? Complete what they say.

Sarah:

Brr ...! Pudding again.

I really _____ . Why isn't there

any ice cream?

Christine:

Ugh ...! Sausages.

I _____ yesterday.

I can't _____ every day.

Joe:

Look at those eggs. I _____ this

morning. I_____ another egg

now.

Tom:

I _____ chocolate pudding. If

you don't want your chocolate pud-

ding, you _____ to me.

Sandra to Kevin:

For me it's chips. I could _____

from morning to night.

Kevin:

What about this fruit salad? I think I'll

_____ . _____ you

_____ fruit salad, too, Sandra?

Die Stellung von Zeit- und Ortsangaben

	Tom	gets up		at 6.30
	He	leaves	home	after breakfast.
Today	he	walks	to school.	
In England	school	starts		at 8.30.
Zeit/Ort			Ort	Zeit

Zeitangaben stehen meist am Ende des Satzes. Wenn sie am Satzanfang stehen, sind sie stärker betont. Auch Ortsangaben können am Satzanfang stehen.

Wenn Zeit- und Ortsangaben zusammentreffen, steht die Ortsangabe immer vor der Zeitangabe.

Training 6: Schools in England

Schools in England are different. Here is some information about schools in England. Put the words in the right order.

1. already go/English pupils/when they are five/to school
2. go to a comprehensive school/most British pupils/when they are eleven
3. when they are 16/school/they can leave
4. school uniform/in many schools/they must wear
5. are blue and grey/the school colours/in Tom's school
6. the school uniforms/in special shops/can buy/the pupils' parents
7. later than in Germany/in most English schools/begin lessons
8. lessons/in the afternoon/most English pupils have/also
9. school cafeterias/many English schools/so/there are lessons also in the afternoon/have
10. lunch/pupils/can have/during break/at the school cafeteria
11. In many English schools/learn/pupils/to cook

Training 7: Tom's timetable

This is Tom's timetable for Monday.   *Now ask Tom*

9.15 – 9.55	Maths	– what subjects he has on Monday.
9.55 –10.35	Maths	– what he has in the first, second … lesson.
10.35 – 10.50	Break	– what he does in the break.
10.50 – 11.30	Biology	– what he does from 1.45 to 2.25.
11.30 – 12.10	Biology	– when and where he sees Jenny.
12.10 – 1.45	Lunch break	– if he has lunch in the school cafeteria.
1.45 – 2.25	Geography	
2.25 – 3.05	English	– when he does his homework.
3.05 – 3.45	German	– where he does his homework.

Example: What subjects do you have on Monday? – Well, on Monday I have …

Die Stellung der Adverbien der Häufigkeit

Unter Adverbien der Häufigkeit versteht man Ausdrücke wie *often, always, sometimes, never, usually* u.a. Sie geben an, wie oft man bestimmte Dinge tut. Im Englischen stehen die Adverbien der Häufigkeit:

a) im *simple present* vor dem Verb,

Tom **usually** does his homework at home.
He **sometimes** forgets his homework.

b) bei Hilfsverben, denen ein Infinitiv oder ein *past participle* folgt, vor dem Infinitiv/*past participle*,

He must **always** help his sister.
She has **never** done his homework.

c) im *simple present* und *simple past* nach den Formen von *to be*, sonst wie unter b).

Timmy isn't **often** ill.
He was **sometimes** ill last year.
But he has **never** been really ill.

 Sometimes kann auch am Satzanfang stehen, wenn es besonders betont ist:
Sometimes Tom forgets his homework.

Training 8: Homework

Put in often, usually, etc.

	who	forget	their homework.
	who	have	forgotten their homework.
	who	do	their homework at school.
	who	have	copied it from their neighbours.
	who	know	what they must do.
There are pupils	who	write	down what they must do.
	who	forget	their homework at home.
	who	do	it on the way to school.
	who	leave	their exercise book at home.
	who	forget	it on the bus.

usually   sometimes   never   usually   often
sometimes   never   always   never   never

Training 9: You and your homework

Answer in full sentence. Use always, often, etc. in your answers.

1. What about your homework? Do you usually do it?
2. When do you usually do it?
3. Where do you do it?
4. Do you often forget it?
5. Why do you sometimes forget it?
6. Do you often copy it from your neighbour?
7. Are you usually busy in the breaks?
8. Does your neighbour/your mum/your dad often help you with your home-work?
9. In what subjects does he or she often help you?
10. Has your teacher ever helped you?

Alexander P. Saccaro

Training
Englische Grammatik
5./6. Schuljahr

Lösungsheft

Ernst Klett Verlag für Wissen und Bildung
Stuttgart · Dresden

Hinweis: Bei den Lösungen wurde nur eine mögliche Antwort angegeben. Sowohl die Langformen (she is, cannot, is not usw.) als auch die Kurzformen (she's, can't isn't usw.) sind als richtig zu betrachten.

Kapitel 1

Training 1

a) There are Mr Mason and his wife on the farm. There are a cock and a few geese, some hens, a cat, a dog and some pigs on the farm, too.

b) *nouns in the singular*   *nouns in the plural*

a farmhouse   farmhouses
a wife   wives
a dog   dogs
a pig   pigs
a cock   cocks
a hen   hens
a goose   geese
a chimney   chimneys
an apple-tree   apple-trees

Training 2

a dog, a pony, a cow, a duck, a goose, a bull, a mouse, a horse

Training 3

There are a lot of men, women and children – presents – two boys – hand – present – teddy – one foot – one arm – one eye – mice – cake

Training 4

are – them – they are – it is – are

Training 5

a) I'm wearing ... (I am wearing)   b) I like ... best.

Kapitel 2

Training 1

1. He is on the farm.
2. She is in the house.
3. He is at school.
4. It is at school, too.
5. He is on his potty.

6. They are on the floor.
7. They are on his bed.
8. She is not at home.
9. She is with her.
10. They are in the park.

Training 2

	Mögliche Antworten:
Where are Tom and Mike?	They are at home/not here/ill ...
Where is your homework?	It's at home/on the desk/on the bus/in my school-bag ...
Where is your English book?	It's in my schoolbag/on the desk/at home/not here.
Where is your book?	It's in my schoolbag/on the desk/at home/not here.
Where is Christine?	She's ill/not here/at home ...
Where is the register?	It's on the desk/in my schoolbag/not here.
Where are they from?	They are from York.
Where are you from?	I'm from York, too.
Where is Kate?	She is in the classroom/at home/not here ...

Training 3

1. I can't find them.
2. I can't find it.
3. I can't see/hear you.
4. I can't see him.
5. I can't see them.
6. I can't find them.

7 I can't find them.
8. I can't see it.
9. I can't find him.
10. I can't see it.
11. I can't see/find it.
12. I can't see/find them.

Training 4

Kate:
I can't see you.

I can't see them.

Timmy:
I'm here.
It's not here. I can't find it.
It's in my bed. I can see it from here.
–

4

Where are they?
Why are you crying?
Are they wet again?
Let's wash them. Help me.

They are in my room.
They are bad trousers.
Yes, they are.

Training 5

Kate: Where are they? Help me to look for them. Are they under your bed?
Timmy: No, they aren't. They aren't there.
Kate: Where are they then? Let me guess. Are they in your bed?
Timmy: No, they aren't in my bed. They are in my teddy's bed.
Kate: Where is it?
Timmy: It's here.
Kate: But why are they in your teddy's bed?
Timmy: It's my teddy who makes them wet, not me.
Kate: Then call your teddy and tell him to help me.

Kapitel 3

Training 1

an English book	a workbook	an exercise book
a German book	a pencil-case	an apple
an empty bottle	a water-pistol	an old sandwich

Training 2

1. He is a milkman.
2. He is a postman.
3. He is a butcher.
4. He is a greengrocer.

5. She is a shop assistant.
6. She is a reporter.
7. He is a fireman.
8. He is a vet.

Training 3

a)
[ðɪ] the old women
[ðɪ] the English children
[ðɪ] the example
[ðə] the yellow apples

[ðə] the young girls
[ðə] the silly answer
[ðə] the bad ideas
[ðɪ] the afternoons

[ðɪ] the American cars
[ðə] the difficult questions
[ðə] the school uniforms
[ðɪ] the empty pages

Training 4

1. Boys like girls.
2. Tom likes Jenny.
3. Do you like the boys in your class?
4. Do you usually like girls more than boys?
5. What about the girls in your class?
6. Which of the boys/girls do you like best?
7. Who is the nicest boy/girl in your class?
8. What's the name of the girl/boy you like best?
9. Are the boys/girls in your class good at English?
10. Are boys as clever as girls?

Training 5

Jenny is not Tom's sister, she is Tom's friend – in Apple Street – Apple Street is – in the north of York – to school by bus – to school by bike – Tom is – all the girls and boys – she likes Tom – the nicest boy – like Tom – likes maths – Maths is the subject – before tests – helps Tom – likes pets

Training 6

Jenny goes to the same school as Tom – takes them to school in the morning – The school they go to is a big school. – a lot of pupils – like school – she likes school – most of the teachers – she can't go to school – stay in bed – a temperature – a cold – a bad headache – a/the doctor – stay in bed

Training 7

Mögliche Antworten:
I can go to Germany by plane/by train ...
I can go to Scotland by train/by car/by taxi/by bike/by motor-bike/on foot ...
I can go to Ireland by plane/by boat ...
I can go to Denmark by plane/by boat ...
I can go to France by plane/by train/by ferry...
I can go to the Isle of Wight by boat/by train ...
I can go to Wales by train/by plane/by bus/by car ...

Kapitel 4

Training 1

1. It's their farm.
2. It's their flat.
3. It's their car.
4. It's his sister.

5. It's her brother.
6. They are his toys.
7. It's his camera.
8. It's her boyfriend.

Training 2

1. It's not your exercise book, it's Kate's. It's her exercise book.
2. ... when you keep it under your bed? What will her teacher say?
3. I think they are his keys.
4. This is not your picture book, it's Kate's. It was her birthday present ...
5. ... here's your teddy, ... your van, ... your telephone. So play with your things now.

Training 3

1. What about your room? Do you like it?
2. Do you clean it or does your mother clean it?
3. What's in your room?
4. Is there anything under your bed?
5. Where do you keep your clothes?
6. Where do you do your homework?
7. Have you got a TV in your room?
8. Have you got posters and photos in your room, too?

Training 4

There are a lot of things – There are books – They are on the chairs – And there is something – It's an old pullover – There are some socks – There are holes in them and they look dirty – There are a lot of photos – that photo over there – It's a photo – It's not a new bike, but its handlebars and its saddle are new.

Training 5

Timmy:
1. Is this your classroom?
2. Is this your class?
3. And that class over there?
4. Is this your chair here?

Tom:
1. This isn't my classroom.
2. Yes, this is my class.
3. That's Kate's class.
4. ... that chair over there, that's Jenny's.

5. What's the name of that fat boy?
6. Is that a teacher over there?
7. But that's a teacher,Tom.

7. Ah yes, that's our English teacher.
8. That's a girl in Kate's class.

Training 6

No, Timmy, this isn't your biro/pen/rubber/ruler. It's Kate's. Look! Your biro/pen/rubber/ruler is over there.

No, Timmy, these aren't your socks/cassettes/keys/pencils/shoes. They are Kate's. Look! Your socks/cassettes/keys/pencils/shoes are over there.

Training 7

1. How much homework ...
2. How much time ...
3. How many minutes ...
4. How many hours ...
5. How many subjects ...

6. How much help ...
7. How many tests ...
8. How many good marks ...
9. How many tests ...
10. How much money ...

Training 8

... too many tests.
... too many bad marks.
... too many teachers.
... too much homework.
... too much work.

... too many questions.
... too many boring subjects.
... too much time indoors.
... so much.

Kapitel 5

Training 1

Timmy's toys
our cat's food
the man's boots
Jenny's dog

the boys' teacher
Kate's friends
the children's books
the Masons' house

the girls' schoolbags
women's clothes
the girls' school uniforms
my parents' car

Training 2

Are these your toys, Tom?	Mögliche Antworten:
Are these your toys, Tom?	No, they aren't. They are my baby brother's.
Is this your girlfriend, Kevin?	No, it isn't. It's Tom's.
Is this your magazine, Jenny?	No, it isn't. It's the girls'.
Is this your cat, Kate?	No, it isn't. It's my mother's.
Is this your homework, Joe?	No, it isn't. It's Kevin's.
Is this your house, Mr Mason?	No, it isn't. It's my grandparents'.
Is this your bike, Kate?	No, it isn't. It's Jenny's.
Is this your room, Tom?	No, it isn't. It's my sister's.
Is this your teddy, Jenny?	No, it isn't. It's Timmy's.
Is this your van, Timmy?	Yes, it is.

Training 3

... Tom's baby brother – one of his favourite toys – he's got (he has got) other toys, too – other things – there's (there is) one of Jenny's letters – there's (there is) an old German book and there's (there is) Kate's ruler – some keys – his parents' keys – there's (there is) a tennis ball – Is it Kevin's or Joe's – It can't be Kate's or Tom's ...

Training 4

Genitiv	Kurzform
... Tom's girlfriend	She's twelve (she is)
it is her grandparents' house	she's only got (she has only got) her parents.
Jenny's other relatives	she's got (she has got) an aunt
Jenny's first visit.	... who's (who is) over sixty and who's got (who has got) a flat

Training 5

the boys' legs	the girl's hands	the windows of the car
the doors of my room	the dog's feet	my neighbour's cat
Kate's books	the children's clothes	the end of school
on the evening of	the light of the moon	Jenny's story
my birthday		

Training 6

Mögliche Lösungen:
a bar of chocolate   a tin of peas

lots of chocolate/food…
a glass of milk/tea
a cup of milk/tea
a plate of strawberries…

a pound of cheese/sausages
a bag of crisps
a packet of cornflakes
a piece of cheese

Training 7

five bags of crisps
three packets of biscuits
five bottles of coke
five bottles of lemonade

three pounds of sausages
two tins of pineapples
five packets of ice cream

Training 8

"Get off that bike – on Tom's bike – they will fall off the bike – So Mike took one hand out of his pocket – not very far from the corner shop to the Masons' flat – the bottles fell off the bike – two bottles of lemonade – to Mrs White's shop – no bottles fell off the bike – both hands out of his pockets – into Tom's room – a telephone call from Jenny's mother – she has just come home from school – greetings from Jenny and from my husband – you will hear from Jenny tomorrow.

Kapitel 6

Training 1

1. They have got a flat.
2. They have got five rooms.
3. Tom has got a room, and Kate has got a room, too.
4. Timmy hasn't got a big room.
5. The Masons have got a car.
6. Tom and Kate haven't got a car, they have got bikes.
7. Timmy hasn't got a bike ...
8. But he has got two big toy cars ...

Training 2

a) I have got a cat, a dog, a teddy, two buckets, a telephone, some toy cars, some picture books etc.
b) I have got ...

Training 3

a) Kate hasn't got a sister/a boyfriend/a car/a teddy/a dog/TV/but she has got two brothers, a lot of friends/a bike/toy cars/a football/a radio.
b) I have got … , but I haven't got …
c) My friend has got …/They have got …

Training 4

a) Has Kate got two brothers/a lot of friends/a bike/toy cars/a football/a radio? Yes, she has.
   Has she got a sister/a boyfriend/a car/a teddy/a dog/TV? No, she hasn't.
b) Have you got a brother/a lot of friends/a bike/a teddy/a football/a radio…?Yes, I have./No, I haven't.

Training 5

Beispiele für Lösungen:
Have you got a car? No, I haven't.
Has your mother got a water-pistol? No, she hasn't.
Has your English teacher got a toy car? No, he hasn't.
Have your friends got a lot of toys? Yes, they have.

Kapitel 7

Training 1

… it is Tom's birthday – He is twelve – all his friends are there – his sister is there – Her name is Kate – She is eleven years old – Only Jenny is not there – Where is she? – She is ill – They are all – it is full of children – They are all hungry – There are a lot of sandwiches – there are some bottles – But one bottle is on the floor – it is broken and there is a pool – And who is in the pool? – It is Timmy …

Training 2

That is Kevin and that is Joe.
They are my best friends.
They are in my class.

And that boy over there is Bill.

He is in my class, too, and he is
very good at maths. In tests he
can be very useful.

That is my sister! Her name is
Kate. All her teachers are very happy
when she is ill. And I am happy when
she is back at school again!

And this is my baby brother.
His name is Timmy. He is three years old.

Training 3

1. No, it isn't.
2. No, she isn't.
3. No, he isn't.
4. No, she isn't.
5. Yes, she is.

6. Yes, it is.
7. Yes, there are.
8. No, they aren't.
9. Yes, they are.
10. Yes, it is.

Weitere Möglichkeiten:
Are all his friends there?
Is Kate there, too?
Is she ten years old?
etc.

Yes, they are.
Yes, she is.
No, she isn't.

Training 4

Is it a thing? No, it isn't.
Is it an animal? No, it isn't.
Is it in this room? No, it isn't.
Is it a toy? No, it isn't.
Is it something nice? No, it isn't.
Is it something terrible? Yes, it is.
It is a woman? No, it isn't.
Is it a man? Yes, it is.
Is he old? Yes, he is.
Is he at our school? Yes, he is.
Is it a teacher? Yes, it is.
Is it our maths teacher? Yes, it is.

Training 5

Who is Jenny?

How old is she?

Is she a nice girl?

Why isn't she here?

Where is she now?

Are her parents at home?

What has she got?

Has she got a temperature?

Has she got brothers and sisters?

Is she from York?

Training 6

1. Is Jenny eleven?
2. Is she a nice girl?
3. Is she your girlfriend?
4. Why isn't she here/at your party?
5. What has she got?
6. Has she got a temperature?
7. Where is she?
8. Where are her parents?
9. Are you unhappy?

Kapitel 8

Training 1

coming, lying, drying, calling, cutting, dancing, drinking, flying, listening, making, getting, playing, putting, running, sitting, swimming, tying, watching

Training 2

1. Mike is taking photos.
2. John is sitting at the table and drinking all the lemonade.
3. Kate is skipping.
4. Tom is ringing up Jenny.
5. Betty is flirting with Kevin.
6. Some boys are playing football.
7. Some girls are dancing in the kitchen.
8. Ann is lying on the floor and watching a film on TV.
9. Jim and Barbara are eating sandwiches.
10. Susan is sitting in a corner and reading a magazine.

Training 3

1. That's not right, Timmy. Mike isn't playing with his camera, he's taking photos.
2. John isn't eating all the sandwiches, he's drinking all the lemonade.
3. Kate isn't hopping around like a rabbit, she's skipping.
4. Tom isn't talking to his teacher, he's ringing up Jenny.
5. Betty isn't talking nonsense to Kevin, she's flirting with him.
6. The boys aren't quarrelling about a ball; they are playing football.
7. The girls aren't running around in the kitchen, they are dancing.
8. Ann isn't lying on the floor because she is ill. She's lying on the floor because she is watching a film on TV.
9. Jim and Barbara aren't making sandwiches, they are eating them.
10. Susan isn't reading your picture book, she's reading a magazine.

Training 4

1. Is Mike really playing with his camera?	Yes, he is.
2. Is John really eating all the sandwiches?	Yes, he is.
3. Is Kate really hopping around like a rabbit?	Yes, she is.
4. Is Tom really talking to his teacher?	Yes, he is.
5. Is Betty really talking nonsense to Kevin?	Yes, she is.
6. Are some boys really quarrelling about a ball?	Yes, they are.
7. Are some girls really running around in the kitchen?	Yes, they are.
8. Is Ann really lying on the floor because she is ill?	Yes, she is.
9. Are Jim and Barbara really making sandwiches?	Yes, they are.
10. Is Susan really reading your picture book?	Yes, she is.

Training 5

– What are you doing, Kate?	I'm skipping.
– Are you talking to your teacher, Tom?	No, I'm talking to Jenny.
– What are you doing with your camera, Mike?	I'm taking photos.
– Are you reading my picture book, Susan?	No, I'm reading a magazine.
– Why are you lying on the floor, Ann?	I'm watching a film.
– What are you doing with the ball?	We are playing football.
– What are you doing in the kitchen?	We are dancing.
– What are you doing, John?	I'm drinking lemonade.
– What are you doing, Jim and Barbera?	We're eating sandwiches.

Training 6

First scene:
When is the party over?

Where are the children going?
What are they?
Who is happy, too?
Where is he?
Where is he lying?
What isn't he doing?
Who is playing with Tom's birthday presents?
Where are they now?

Second scene:
Where is Timmy still lying?
What has he got in his hand?
What is he drawing?

Third scene:
Who is coming upstairs?
What is he shouting?
What is he doing?
What is he opening?

Kapitel 9

Training 1

1. He needn't go to school.
2. He can go to kindergarten.
3. He can play with other children there.
4. Must he go there every day?
5. No, he needn't.
6. Can/may he go there alone?
7. No, he can't/may not/mustn't.
8. Can/may he take his bike?
9. No, he can't/may not/mustn't.
10. Must Tom fetch him in the afternoon?
11. Yes, he must fetch him on Thursdays and Fridays.

Training 2

1. No, that's wrong. Kate can go to her room.
2. No, that's wrong. She can/must help her mother.

3. No, that's wrong. Tom must help his mother to wash up the dishes and to clean the kitchen floor, but he needn't clean Kate's room.
4. No, that's wrong. He must help to wash them up.
5. That's right.
6. That's wrong. He needn't clean them.
7. That's right. Timmy can help him with the dishes.
8. That's wrong. He needn't clean it.
9. That's wrong. He mustn't drop them.
10. That's right. He can stay up a little longer.

Training 3

Tom	Jenny's mother
1. Can/may I talk to Jenny, please?	Sorry, Tom, you can't/may not.
2. Can Jenny come tomorrow?	No, she can't. She can't/may not/mustn't get up.
3. Must she stay in bed all day?	Yes, she must.
4. Must she take medicine?	No, she needn't.
5. Can/may I see her this afternoon?	No, you can't/may not see her today. She must go to the doctor's.

Training 4

1. I mustn't go to school.
2. I must stay in bed.
3. I mustn't watch too much TV.
4. I must take my temperature every day.
5. I must take my medicine.
6. I must come to his surgery again on Monday at 4 o'clock.
7. I mustn't play with my friends.

Training 5

She must take her medicine.
She mustn't ride on her bike.
She mustn't go to school.
She needn't do her homework.
She can ring up her friends.
She can write letters.

She can watch TV.
She can read a book.
She needn't/mustn't clean her room.
She needn't/mustn't help her mother.
She can listen to music.
She mustn't play football.

Training 6

1. A good patient must do what the doctor tells him/her.
2. A good patient must tell the doctor what he/she has got.
3. A good patient must take medicine.
4. A good patient must stay in bed when he/she is ill.
5. A good patient needn't clean the doctor's car.
6. A good patient mustn't forget his/her appointment.
7. Correct
8. A good patient must listen to his/her doctor.
9. A good patient needn't clean the doctor's surgery.

Training 7

1. No, you needn't.
2. No, you needn't.
3. Yes, you must.
4. No, you can't.
5. Yes, you can.
6. Yes, you must.
7. Yes, they may, ...
8. Yes, you may.
9. Yes, you must.

Training 8

– Are you very ill?	Yes, I am.
– Must you stay in bed?	Yes, I must.
– Must you stay indoors all day?	Yes, I must.
– May you get up for an hour or two?	Yes, I may.
– Have you got a temperature?	Yes, I have.
– Can you go to school on Thursday?	No, I can't.
– Are you happy that you needn't go to school?	Yes, I am.
– Are your teachers happy, too?	No, they aren't.

Training 9

Shall I do the shopping for you?
Shall I clean the rooms?
Shall I go to the chemist's?
Shall I get your medicine?
Shall I open the window?
Shall I look after my brother/sister?

Shall I cook the meals?
Shall I do the washing-up?
Shall I make your bed?
Shall I make you some tea?
Shall I ring up the doctor?

Kapitel 10

Training 1

1. He gets up ...
2. Then he washes and puts on his clothes.
3. Then he goes down ...
4. There he has breakfast.
5. Then he looks for his schoolbag.
6. After that he leaves the house.
7. Then he goes to the bus stop.
8. He usually takes the bus ...
9. He arrives ...

Training 2

a)
1. Mike and Tom play football ...
2. Sam eats his sandwiches.
3. Sandra does her English homework.
4. Anne talks to Betty.
5. John copies his homework ...
6. Kevin runs around ...
7. Bob and David make a lot of noise ...
8. Pam cleans the board.
9. Jane and Sharon write letters.

b) Mögliche Antworten:
1. I do my homework.
2. I learn English.
3. I talk to my neighbour.
4. I clean the board.
5. I sing a song.

Training 3

1. They don't get up in the morning.
2. They don't have an early breakfast.
3. Mr Brown doesn't wash his car.
4. Mrs Brown doesn't do the cooking.
5. Often, their children don't go to school.
6. They don't like school.
7. Helen doesn't like her teachers.
8. She doesn't do her homework.

Training 4

Tom likes bananas, but he doesn't like oranges.
He likes Jenny, but he doesn't like Ben.
Jenny and Kate like volleyball, but they don't like tennis.
They like sports, but they don't like all sports.
Timmy likes cornflakes, but he doesn't like tea.
He likes dogs, but he doesn't like cats.
Mike likes photos, but he doesn't like comics.

He likes music, but he doesn't like singing.
The Browns don't like work, but they like sleeping.
They don't like books, but they like TV.

Training 5

Mögliche Lösungen:
I like tennis, but my mother doesn't.
I don't like maths, but my neighbour does.
My friends like pop music, but my parents don't.
My parents don't like Kate, but I do.
etc.

Training 6

– Do you like it here?
– Does your mother like York?
– Do you like English?
– Do you like school?
– Do you play hockey?

– Do you go to school by bike?
– Do you like sports?
– Does your sister go to our school, too?
– Do you play an instrument?
– Does your father work in York?

Training 7

1. Do you like your class?
2. Do you like all the subjects?
3. Do you like maths?
4. Do you like all the teachers?
5. Do you often forget your homework?
6. Do you come to school by bus?
7. Do you come to school by bike in winter, too?
8. Do you play football?
9. Do your parents live in York, too?
10. Do you do your homework in the afternoon?

Training 8

1. Where do you live?
2. When do you get up in the morning?
3. When does your mother get up?
4. What do you have for breakfast?
5. Why don't you like cornflakes?
6. When do your parents leave the house?

I live in ...
I get up at ...
She gets up at ...
I have ... for breakfast.
I don't like them because ...
They leave the house at ...

7. When do they come home again?   They come home again at ...
8. How do you get to school?   I get to school by ...
9. Why don't you take the bus?   I don't take it because ...
10. What do you do in the afternoon?   In the afternoon, I ...
11. What games do you like?   I like ...
12. What do you do in the evening?   In the evening, I ...
13. When do you go to bed?   I go to bed at ...
14. When do you switch off the light?   I switch off the light at ...
15. When do your parents go to bed?   They go to bed at ...

Training 9

a) 1. When do you get up?
   2. When do you start work?
   3. When do you leave the house?
   4. What do you drive?
   5. Who do you collect from the villages?
   6. Where do you take them?
   7. When does school start?
   8. When do you fetch them?
   9. Where do you take them?
   10. What do you clean then?
   11. What do you often find in the bus?

b) I get up at 5.30, because work starts at seven o'clock. I leave my house at 6.30.
   I drive a school bus. I collect the children from the villages and take them to
   school. School starts at a quarter to nine. In the afternoon I fetch them from
   school and take them home again. Then I clean the bus. I often find things in the
   bus.

Training 10

Where does Mike live now?
What doesn't he like?
How does he go to school?
When does his mother drive him to school?
When does the first lesson begin?
When does he get up?
Where does he usually arrive at 8.30?
Why does he have lunch at school?
What do they play together until 6 or 7 o'clock?
What do they do?

Kapitel 11

Training 1

1. Mike usually gets up at 7, but today he is still in bed. He is sleeping.
2. He usually has breakfast at 7.30, but today he is still lying in bed.
3. He often has little time to spend in the bathroom, but this morning he is taking a bath.
4. He usually puts on his school uniform, but today he is wearing his other clothes.
5. He usually has lunch at school, but today he is having lunch at home.
6. Mike usually helps his mother with the dishes. His father is washing the dishes.
7. His parents usually work in the afternoon, ... They are going for a walk.
   Do you know why? Well, it's Sunday.

Training 2

Mögliche Antworten:
On Sundays I usually get up late/go for a walk/do my homework.
On Sundays I often watch TV/ring up my friends/play football/write letters.
On Sundays I sometimes cook lunch/help Mum and Dad/brush my shoes.
On Sundays I never clean my room/clean my bike/go to school/learn English.

Training 3

1. Mike is taking a picture of his new school. He likes taking pictures.
2. He doesn't only take pictures of schools, he takes pictures of everything. Here he is taking a picture of Tom and Jenny.
3. He always puts his pictures in an album. Look! He is putting a picture in his album now.
4. He has already got a lot of albums. He keeps them in his room.

Training 4

This is Dad. He is sitting in his bus.

This is Dad again. He is cleaning the bus.

This is our house. We live there now.

This is Mum. She is leaving the house. She always leaves at 8.

This is our garden. Look! Mum is working in it. She likes her garden.

This is our corner shop. Mum works there. She sells groceries.

Training 5

First they break the eggs and put them in a bowl.
Then they add some milk, salt and pepper.
Then they stir the eggs.
Next they look for a frying pan.
Then they put fat in it.
Then they put the pan on the oven.
After that they put everything in the frying pan and stir two or three times.
Then they put the scrambled eggs on a plate.
Then they take the eggs upstairs and eat them.

Training 6

a) 1. When do you usually get up?
   2. When do you usually wash?
   3. When do you usually have breakfast?
   4. When do you usually get in your car?
   5. When do you usually open the surgery?
   6. When do you usually examine sick animals?
   7. When do you usually have lunch/Where do you usually have lunch?
   8. When do you usually leave the restaurant?
   9. When do you usually have a cup of tea?
   10. When do you usually close the door of the surgery?
   11. When do you usually get home?

b) Mr Mason usually gets up at seven o'clock every morning. Then he washes and
   has breakfast. After that he gets in his car. He opens his surgery at 8.30. He ex-
   amines sick animals between 9 and 12. Then he has lunch at a restaurant. He
   usually leaves the restaurant at 13.45. At 5 he usually has a cup of tea. He closes
   the door of his surgery at 5.30. He usually gets home at 6.

Training 7

Mögliche Antworten:
I get up at ..., then I wash and have breakfast. Then I go to school. I usually get home
at ... In the afternoon I first ..., then I ... After that I ... In the evenings I usually ... I go to
bed at ...

Training 8

... the sun is shining – the Masons are still sitting at the breakfast table – nobody is doing any work – Mr Mason isn't looking after animals – Mrs Mason – she works in a hospital as a nurse – isn't looking after her patients.
... The Masons always have a late breakfast – she is sleeping – Mr Mason asks – "What is she doing in her room?" – So Timmy goes to Kate's room – he opens the door and sees – he tries to wake her up, but Kate doesn't listen, so Timmy goes back and tells his dad that Kate is still sleeping – Mr Mason says – if she doesn't want to get up – Timmy fetches Tom's water-pistol and goes to Kate's room – somebody is shouting in an angry voice ...

Kapitel 12

Training 1

Dear Jenny,
I hope we can see each other this afternoon. I have got a lot of homework to do, but I think I can come ... I hope I can come. I really want to see you again. You are the nicest girl I know. I am always thinking of you. You know I like you.

Training 2

Mögliche Antworten:
Jenny doesn't begin to cry.
She must laugh.
She writes a letter, too, and shows it to her neighbours.
They all begin to laugh.
She isn't very angry.
She doesn't go home immediately.

Training 3

Jenny isn't ten years old, she is twelve.
Her parents have got a flat. They haven't got a house.
Her father has got a van. He hasn't got a car.

She doesn't go to school by bus. She goes to school by bike.
She likes maths, but she doesn't like English.
She has got a good maths teacher, but her English teacher is awful.
She doesn't like all the boys in her class, but she likes Tom.

She is sometimes late, but she isn't late very often.
She likes music, but she doesn't like singing.
She can play a lot of games, but she can't play football.
She is good at volleyball, but she is bad at swimming.

Training 4

Mögliche Antworten:

I'm ..., I'm not ...

I've got ..., but I haven't got ...

My parents have got ..., but we haven't got ...

We have got ..., but we haven't got ...

She is ..., she isn't ...

She has got ..., but she hasn't got ...

Her parents ...

They have got ..., but they haven't got ...

I go to school by ...

I like ..., but I don't like ...

I have got ..., but I haven't got ...

I don't like ..., but I like ...

She goes to ...

She likes ..., but she doesn't like ...

She has got ..., but she hasn't got ...

She doesn't like ..., but she likes ...

I am often/never ..., but sometimes I ...

I like ..., but I don't like ...

I can play ..., but I can't ...

I am good at ..., but I am bad at ...

She is often/never ..., but sometimes I ...

She likes ..., but she doesn't like ...

She can play ..., but she can't play ...

She is good at ..., but she is bad at ...

Training 5

Mögliche Antworten:

– That's wrong. Some of them do, but others don't.
– That's wrong. Good pupils aren't silly.
– That's wrong. Sometimes they forget things, too.
– That's wrong. Some of them have a lot of friends, others don't.
– That's wrong. Some of them make their teachers angry, too.
– That's wrong again. Good pupils talk in lessons, too.
– That's wrong. Good pupils aren't unhappy, but sometimes bad pupils are.
– That's wrong again. Some of them are bad at sports, but not all of them.
– That's wrong, too. Some of them do, but not all of them work too much.
– This is right. Good pupils usually do their homework.

Training 6

– Are you often alone?
– Do you like your parents?
– Have you got any friends?

– Have you got any hobbies?
– Do your parents often play with you?
– Have you got anybody to talk to?

– Do you watch a lot of TV?
– Are most of your teachers nice?
– Are you often afraid?

– Do you often cry?
– Can you do what you want?
– Are your parents often out in the evening?

Training 7

– Do you like school?
– Do you often forget your homework?
– Are you doing your homework now?
– Is your mum helping you now?
– Do your parents often help you?
– Have you got nice teachers?
– Do they like you?
– Do they give you a lot of homework?
– Can you talk during lessons?
– May you eat chewing gum in the English lessons?
– Have you got a school magazine at your school?
– Do you read it?
– Do you find it interesting?

Training 8

– Do you find everything boring?
– Do you often sleep during lessons?

– Are you often ill for tests?
– Do you only like sports?

– Are you often late?

– Do you listen only when your teacher gets angry?
– Do you often forget things?

– Can you sit still?
– Do you talk all the time?
– Can you listen?

– Do you do your homework?

Training 9

1. No, it isn't.
2. No, it isn't.
3. No, he isn't.
4. No, they aren't.
5. Yes, they are.
6. Yes, he is.

7. Yes, he does.
8. Yes, they are.
9. Yes, he is.
10. Yes, they do.
11. Yes, they do.
12. No, it isn't. It's a motor-bike.

Training 10

1. Who is Tom's girlfriend?
2. Who is from Leeds?
3. What have they got?
4. Who is sometimes strict?
5. Who can't she always see?
6. What must she tell her parents?
7. Who must be back early?
   When must she be back?
8. When mustn't she be out?
9. What is ringing?
10. Where is Tom?

Training 11

1. What have you got?
2. What is it?
3. What do you like/What do you do?
4. What must you buy for it?
5. Where must I go?
6. What must I lend you?
7. What do you want to buy?
9. What is very bad?
10. Who can't you understand?

Training 12

1. How old is he?
2. Where does he sleep?
3. When do you usually get up?
4. What do you do then?
5. What does he usually have for breakfast?
6. When do you take him for a walk?
7. When do you go to work?
8. Where do you take him then?
9. How long does he stay there?
10. Where do you play?
11. What do you try to teach him?
12. What do you do in the evening?
13. What films does he like?
14. Why does he like westerns?

26

Training 13

1. When can I see you again?
2. Where can we meet again?
3. How long can you stay?
4. When must you be back?
5. Why must you be back so early?
6. When must you help your mother?
7. What must you do?

Kapitel 13

Training 1

I think the weather will be nice.
I hope we'll spend a nice day together.
I don't think it will rain,
Perhaps the sun will shine.
I hope the water won't be too cold.
If the water isn't too cold, we'll go for a swim.
We will spend the afternoon there.
I hope you'll have a good time.

Training 2

Jenny:
When will we be there?
Will we need a warm pullover?
Will you buy us an ice cream?
Kevin:
Will we have lunch on the beach?
Will we play games on the beach?
Peter:
What games will we play?
Will we be allowed to walk around on our own?
Susan:
Will we have time enough to go shopping?
When will we be back?
Will the maths teacher come with us?

Training 3

a) She hopes that the weather will be nice.
   Perhaps it won't rain.

She is sure that they will have lots of fun.
She hopes that her friends will go, too.
She is sure that there will be a lot of interesting things to see.
She thinks that her pocket money will be enough.
She hopes that there won't be too many teachers.
She hopes that there won't be any homework for the next day.

b) Mögliche Antworten:
I hope the bus won't have a breakdown.
I hope our teachers will leave us alone.
I hope we won't have to visit that terrible museum.
Perhaps I'll find a nice present for my friend.
etc.

Training 4

Mögliche Antworten:
If the coach is late, they won't leave at 8'clock.
If the coach breaks down, the driver won't be happy.
If it rains all day, they won't go to the beach.
If the sun doesn't shine, they won't go for a swim.
If some of the children are late, their teacher will be angry.
If Mr Benson is ill, there will be no excursion.
If Kate loses her pocket money, she will be unhappy.
If they take the wrong road, they will be late.

Training 5

Mögliche Lösungen:
When they are on the beach, they will take off their clothes/they will play games/they will go for a swim//they will splash Mr Benson with water/they will have a picnic on the beach/they will be very noisy/they will run around/they will rush into the water/play softball/look for shells.

Training 6

Catherine: I'll buy something to drink, too.
Jim: No problem. I'll help you.

Helen: I'll buy some, too.
Ronny: Well, then, I'll have a sandwich, too.

28

Training 7

a) 1. ... she is going to work harder.
   2. ... so she is going to help her.
   3. ... so she isn't going to invite him.
   4. ... She is going to write him this afternoon.
   5. ... Her parents are going to buy her a new bike.
   6. ... What is she going to do? Well, she is going to clean it.
   7. ... She is going to go to the seaside.
   8. ... She is going to spend her holiday there.

b) 1. What are you going to do about your tests, Kate? Are you going to work harder?
   2. What are you going to do, Jenny? Are you going to help Kate?
   3. What are you going to do, Kate? Are you going to invite Ronny?
   4. What are you going to do this afternoon, Helen? Are you going to spend it with Ben?
   5. What are your parents going to do, Linda? Are they going to buy you a new bike?
   6. What are you going to do with your room, Betty? Are you going to clean it?
   7. What are you going to do in your holidays, Mary? Are you going to go to the seaside?
   8. What are you going to do there? Are you going to spend your holiday there?

Training 8

1. If the weather is fine, we'll play in the garden.
2. I think everybody will like that.
3. But I hope Ronny won't come. I'm not going to invite him.
4. Perhaps Jenny will help me.
5. I hope Tom will help me with the lemonade. I will ask him when I see him.
6. Who is going to buy/will buy all the rest?
7. Well, I'll ask Mum if she ... Perhaps he will be tired tired when he gets back.

Training 9

I'm going to ring up my friends.
I'm going to invite them.
I'll ask them if they can come.
I'm going to go to a supermarket to buy things.
I'll ask Dad if he can help me.
Perhaps he'll have time to help me.

I hope Mum will help me, too.
She will make chips and sausages for us if I ask her.
I hope she will let us use the dining-room if it rains.

Training 10

1. Tomorrow we will (are going to) write an English test.
2. I hope it won't be too difficult.
3. I hope my neighbour will help me.
4. Perhaps I'll get a good mark then.
5. I'm going to ask her tonight if she wants to help me.
6. If she helps me, I'll give her a bar of chocolate.
7. But I'll only give it to her if I my mark is good.
8. If my mark is bad, I'll eat the bar of chocolate myself.

Kapitel 14

Training 1

a) lived, given; carried, played; said, lain; showed, felt; caught, thought; brought, told; left, bet; spent, stood; written, taken

b) to pay, to teach; to choose, to fall; to lose, to drop; to throw, to try; to feed, to buy

Training 2

– They have booked a place for July.
– They have written to the local tourist office.
– They have bought a new road map.
– They have had a look at it.
– They have tried to find out the best route.
– They have begun to check their caravan.
– They have bought a new bottle of gas.
– They have cleaned the water tank.
– They have checked the tyres.
– They have repaired the rear window.

Training 3

We have washed the caravan, but we haven't cleaned the floor yet.
We have cleaned the windows, but we haven't made the beds yet.

We have put in some food, but we haven't bought a new frying pan yet.
We have taken Pete's tennis racket, but we haven't bought new tennis balls yet.
We have told the neighbours to look after the flowers, but we haven't given them a key yet.
We have put in Timmy's teddy, but we haven't bought a new picture book yet.

Training 4

Have you put my telephone in the caravan?
Have you taken away my pencils?
Have you bought a new picture book for me?
Have you put it in the caravan?
Have you bought some chocolate?
Have you packed my swimming things?
Have you seen my teddy?
Have you found my red toy car?

Training 5

Mrs Mason:	Yes, we have.	Tom:	Yes, I have.
Tom:	Yes, I have.	Tom:	Yes, he has.
Kate:	Yes, I have.	Timmy:	No, I haven't.
All:	Yes, we have.	All:	No, we haven't.
		Timmy:	No, we can't.

Training 6

Mögliche Fragen:

Have you ever been to a caravan site?	No, I haven't. I have never been to a caravan site.
Have you ever cleaned a caravan?	No, I haven't. I haven't cleaned a caravan yet.
Has your father ever had an accident?	No, he hasn't. He hasn't had an accident yet.
Has your sister ever been to England?	No, she hasn't. She hasn't been to England yet.
Have your friends ever slept in a caravan?	No, they haven't. They have never slept there.

etc.

Training 7

1. The Masons have already packed everything.
2. They have put all their things in the caravan.
3. They have already done 100 kilometres.
4. But they have not arrived at their camping site yet.
5. Timmy has not been sick yet.
6. He has not had breakfast yet.
7. But he has already been on his potty four times.

Training 8

1. I know what you told me.
2. Here it is.
3. He is angry now.

4. I know it.
5. I don't know it.
6. It is/looks dirty.

Training 9

Jenny has kissed him goodbye.

He has found them again.

He has put it in the fridge.

They have packed everything.

Somebody has forgotten to shut it.

The Masons have left.

Kapitel 15

Training 1

Regular verbs: say, stop, play, cry, carry

Irregular verbs: lead, read, sit, write, tear, catch, set, ride, hear, think, swim, feed, bring, teach, let, meet, lose, get, hit, hide, fly, break

Training 2

The Masons wanted to leave – it was quite late when they got off – Kate was still tired – Tom wanted to finish a letter – Timmy's potty was missing – nobody knew where it was – When they were all in the car again, somebody saw that a window was still open – Mr Mason got out of the car, went into the house again and shut it – When he came back, Timmy wanted to go – So Mr Mason got out of the car – and carried Timmy to the bathroom – When they were back, they heard the telephone – So Tom got out of the car and ran into the house – he was not fast enough – When he arrived, the line was dead – finally they were ready to leave

Training 3

They finally left at 11 o'clock. Their first stop was at 11.30 because Timmy was sick. They stopped again at 12.15 because Timmy was sick again. At 1 o'clock they had lunch, but when they left, they forgot Timmy's teddy. At 2 o'clock they got in their car again and drove on. As Mr Mason took a short cut, they lost two hours. They arrived at 6 o'clock at the camping site. There they tried to put up a tent for Tom, but it collapsed. They had supper at 8. At 9 they all went to bed because they were very tired.

Training 4

The first night Timmy did not sleep very well. He didn't have his teddy and it was not quiet enough at the camping site. At home he didn't sleep in the same bed with Kate. She didn't leave him enough room and she didn't want him in "her" bed. So Timmy wasn't warm enough. He didn't have nice dreams and was not happy that night.

Training 5

Mögliche Antworten:
Timmy was not sick anymore. He felt better.
Tom didn't do any homework. He wrote a letter to Jenny.
Kate didn't stay in the caravan. She looked for new friends.
Mr Mason didn't lie on the beach. He went for a walk.
Mrs Mason didn't cook in the caravan. She bought a new teddy for Timmy.

Training 6

1. Did you ...?   Yes, I did.
2. Did you ...?   Yes, I did.
3. Did you ...?   Yes, I did.
4. Was it ...?   No, it wasn't.
5. Did you ...?   Yes, I did.

6. Did you ...?   Yes, I did.
7. Were there ...?   Yes, there were.
8. Did you ...?   No, I didn't.
9. Were they ...?   No, they weren't.
10. Where they ...?   Yes, they were.

Training 7

Mögliche Fragen:
– Where is Timmy?

– How did it happen?
– Where did it happen?

- What happened?
- Is Timmy hurt?
- Did he break anything?
  etc.

- Did anybody help him?
- Did anybody call a doctor?
- How far is it from here?

Training 8

- Did it hurt, Timmy?
- How did the accident happen?
- Why didn't you see the stone?
- Did you fall on your arm?
- Did you cry?
- When did you break your arm?
- Was your teddy all right?
- Who helped you?
- Was anybody with you?

Training 9

- He was allowed to play with his teddy.
- He was allowed to draw a picture with his right arm.
- He was allowed to talk to the nurses./He could talk to the nurses.
- He didn't have to make his bed.
- He wasn't allowed to run around in the room.
- He was allowed to look at his picture book.
- He had to be careful with his arm.
- He had to keep his arm still.
- He didn't have to clean the room.
- He wasn't allowed to play in the corridor.
- He didn't have to stay in bed all day.
- He had to eat his meals.

Training 10

Mögliche Lösungen:
- Were you allowed to play with your teddy? – Yes, I was.
- Were you allowed to draw pictures with your right arm? – Yes, I was.
- Could you talk to the nurses? – Yes, I could.
- Did you have to make your bed? – No, I didn't.
- Were you allowed to run around in the room? – No, I wasn't.
- Were you allowed to look at your picture book? – Yes, I was.
- Did you have to be careful with your arm? – Yes, I did.

– Did you have to keep your arm still? – Yes, I did.
– Did you have to clean your room? – No, I didn't.
– Were you allowed to play in the corridor? – No, I wasn't.
– Did you have to stay in bed all day? – No, I didn't.
– Did you have to eat your meals? – Yes, I did.

Training 11

... the Masons were allowed to take Timmy home – They didn't have to leave the camping site – that Timmy wasn't allowed to do – He didn't have to stay in the caravan – but he had to be careful – he wasn't allowed to play any wild games – he wasn't allowed to swim – he didn't have to take any medicine – they didn't have to worry – they had to see ...

Kapitel 16

Training 1

First Tom sent Kate back to their parents.
So Kate ran back to the caravan.
Then she told her parents all about Timmy's accident.
Then Mrs Mason phoned a doctor.
When the doctor arrived, she examined Timmy.
After that she called an ambulance.
When the ambulance arrived, the ambulance men put Timmy on a stretcher.
After that they drove him to the hospital.

Training 2

When Timmy had a accident,
a woman was reading a magazine,
a man was lying in a deckchair,
some people were swimming,
two children were playing with a ball,
a girl was putting on her clothes,
a boy was listening to a radio,
a family was having a picnic

Training 3

Mögliche Fragen:

What were you doing when
the accident happened?
Were you having a swim?
Were you playing on the beach?
Were you reading a magazine?
etc.

Were you sleeping?
Were you watching the sea/
the boys/the girls?
Were you listening to your radio?

Training 4

Mögliche Antworten:
When poor Timmy broke his arm,
– Mr Mason was drinking beer with their neighbours,
– Mr Mason was smoking and talking,
– his wife was lying in the sun,
– she was just having breakfast,
– Kate was just getting up,
– Tom was writing a letter,
– nobody was looking after him.

Training 5

1. While they were sitting in the waiting-room, the door opened. A man came in.
2. He was wearing a bandage round his head.
3. He said good morning. Then he sat down and looked for a newspaper.
4. He opened the newspaper and began to read.
5. While he was reading his newspaper, a nurse came in.
6. She told Mr Mason and Mrs Mason to follow her.
7. She led them to the room where Timmy was waiting.
8. There a doctor was talking to Timmy.
9. Timmy was asking him a lot of questions.
10. When the doctor saw them, he called them to Timmy's bed.
11. Timmy was laughing. He was happy that he could go home.
12. They thanked the doctor and packed Timmy's things. Then they left the hospital.

Training 6

I was playing football when I fell to the ground and broke my arm.
I was climbing a rock when I slipped.
I slipped when I was having a shower. I broke three ribs.

I was cleaning the windows when the ladder broke. I fell onto the floor.
I was lying in my deckchair when it collapsed.
I was doing my homework when I fell asleep. I fell off the chair.

Training 7

Timmy still had to be very careful – he couldn't go for a swim – everybody had to keep him busy – Tom often read ghost stories to him – Timmy's favourite story was about an American family who wanted to buy – When they came to the castle, the sun was not shining – it was raining and thunder sounded again and again – When they entered the castle – a flash of lightning filled – and there was lightning – when they came down – they saw blood – the next night they heard – when Mr Otis opened – he saw – long hair fell from his head – his eyes were like fire ...

Kapitel 17

Training 1

1. When did you come back?
2. Where did you go?
3. Did you like your stay there?
4. Have you ever been to Italy?
5. Did you do anything for school as Old Misery told you?
6. Did you play tennis in the holidays?
7. How many postcards did you write?
8. Where did you buy these shoes?
9. What was the weather like? Did it rain a lot?
10. Have you already seen Mike?

Training 2

Mögliche Antworten:
– I came back ...
– I went to ... /I stayed ...
– Yes, I did/No, I didn't.
– Yes, I have/No, I haven't.
– Yes, I did/No, I didn't.
– Yes, I did/No, I didn't.
– I wrote ... postcards/I didn't write any postcards.
– I bought them ...

– It was fine/hot/very warm/lovely. Yes, it did/No, it didn't.
– No, I haven't.

Training 3

We stayed there for two weeks.
We always went swimming there.
We had an accident, but we haven't repaired it yet.

We visited the castle. Did you know Charles I was a prisoner there?
I played with him a lot. We often went to the beach and had a swim together.
We played with her sometimes.

Training 4

– I haven't been late any more. I was only late the first day.
– I have nearly always listened to my teachers.
– I have never again played during lessons.
– I have only sometimes talked to my neighbour.
– I haven't forgotten my books again. I forgot them only yesterday.
– I have done my homework in all subjects. I only didn't do it last Monday.
– I have usually gone home immediately after school.
– I have written better tests and got good marks.
– I have learned more German. Yesterday I nearly spent ten minutes on my German
  homework.
– I haven't watched so much TV. Yesterday I only watched one hour.

Training 5

– We came back yesterday.
– I often went swimming.
– I got to know a German boy.
– I met Mike in the holidays.
– I talked a lot of German.
– We had an accident.
– I didn't do any homework in the holidays.
– I have become really fat.
– I ate too much in the holidays.
– We visited a lot of castles in the holidays.

Training 6

In the holidays we visited Carisbrooke Castle. Carisbrooke Castle is an old castle. It is famous, too, because Charles I was a prisoner there ... People say that he hasn't found peace yet and that his ghost is still walking there.

When we got there, the sky was very dark. When we walked through the entrance, it began to rain. So we went into the castle, but it was very dark in there, too. There were lots of strange noises. Suddenly a door opened. When I looked there, I saw something green. It was coming towards me. I ran out of the building and told everything to my parents. They didn't believe me. They just laughed at me.

Two days after the holidays were over we had to go home again. That night I went to bed early, but woke up at midnight. There was a strange noise again. I saw something green. It was sitting at my desk, but before I could say anything, it was gone. I soon forgot this, but two weeks later I woke up again. I saw a green shadow at my desk again. It was writing something in an exercise book. I was very afraid and did not move. Five minutes later it was gone. As it didn't come back, I got up and went to the desk. There I saw my exercise book. It was open, but there was a note in the book: This is what the ghost told me and that's why I did not do any homework last Tuesday.

Training 7

Mögliche Antworten:
I couldn't do any homework because
– my neighbour was ill.
– I left my book at school.
– my mother/father/sister was ill yesterday.
– I felt so ill in the afternoon.
– my pen did not work.
– I forgot my schoolbag.
– my exercise book was full.
– I had to repair my bike.
– my mother had no time to do it.

I can't show you my homework because
– I have left it on the bus/at home.
– I have forgotten my schoolbag.
– my baby brother/sister has eaten it.
– my baby brother has made a plane out of it.

Kapitel 18

Training 1

Mögliche Antworten:
My friend? He is tall and thin, but he is very strong, too.
My friend? She is fat and small, but she is exciting, too.
My sister? She is nice and funny, but she can be difficult, too.
My brother? He noisy and fat, but he but he can be nice, too.

Training 2

Mögliche Antworten:
Comics are boring/interesting/wonderful/exciting/fantastic ...
Films are boring/funny/interesting/exciting/wonderful ...
Books are interesting/exciting/wonderful/fantastic/funny...
Football is exciting/boring/fantastic/dangerous/interesting/difficult ...
TV is boring/bad/exciting/fantastic/dangerous/interesting ...
English tests are wonderful/fantastic/exciting/funny/interesting ...
Boys are exciting/dangerous/wonderful/clever/intelligent ...
Teachers are loud/boring/dangerous/strange/crazy ...
Baby brothers/sisters are loud/fat/noisy/boring ...
Pop music is beautiful/fantastic/wonderful/loud ...
Girls are noisy/difficult/boring/beautiful ...

Training 3

a funny girl	– a boring girl
an old town	– a new/modern town
a small boy	– a tall boy
a good mark	– a bad mark
a boring film	– an exciting/interesting film
a fast runner	– a slow runner
a bad driver	– a good driver
a clever pupil	– a silly pupil
a quiet boy	– a noisy boy
a happy child	– an unhappy child
a difficult text	– an easy text
a silly person	– an intelligent person
a terrible story	– a nice story
a rich man	– a poor man

40

Training 4

good, better, the best; careful, more careful, the most careful; noisy, noisier, the noisiest; fat, fatter, the fattest; powerful, more powerful, the most powerful; nice, nicer, the nicest; intelligent, more intelligent, the most intelligent; heavy, heavier, the heaviest; dangerous, more dangerous, the most dangerous; quick, quicker, the quickest.

Training 5

Mögliche Antworten:
Tom's dad is the tallest in the family. He is taller than Grandpa and he is taller than his wife. Tom is the tallest of the children. Kate and Timmy are smaller than Tom. Timmy is the smallest of them all.

Training 6:

Susan: I think tennis is more difficult than swimming.
Betty: No, it isn't, but it's more expensive.
Susan: More expensive? I think swimming is as expensive as tennis.

Susan: I think English is nicer than German.
Betty: No, it isn't, but it's more useful.
Susan: More useful? I think it's as useful as English.

Susan: I think comics are funnier than books.
Betty: No, they aren't, but books are more interesting than comics.
Susan: More interesting? I think comics are as interesting as books.

Training 7

Susan:
I think he's the tallest boy in our class.
He must be the strongest boy ...
It has got the same colour as your hair.
I need somebody who is cleverer than Tom. You know, at maths Tom is even worse than me.
Anne told me his photos are the best photos she has ever seen.

Jane:
No, I think David is taller than him.
He is even nicer than Tom.
... or you'll get a prize for the silliest question.
He looks a bit silly, but perhaps he is better at maths than he looks.

Training 8

1. Has your English become better?
2. Let's hope it hasn't become worse.
3. Is the number of mistakes in your English tests smaller or bigger now?
4. Were the exercises very boring?
5. Were they more interesting than in your textbook?
6. Were they as boring as in your textbook?
7. Or were they worse?
8. Was the grammar clear enough?
9. Or was the grammar in your textbook easier?
10. We hope that you didn't find things too difficult.

Kapitel 19

Training 1

Mögliche Antworten:
Before I go to school, I usually do my homework.
When I don't want to go to school, I tell my mum that I am ill.
When it's too cold to get up, I stay in bed.
When I am late, I don't have breakfast.
When I must go to bed, I still read an hour or two.
Before I get up, I often think that it is too early to get up.
Before I have breakfast, I usually wash.
When I go to bed, I switch off the lights.
When I can't find my homework, I get angry.

Training 2

On Monday, I am going to play table tennis with Tom at 4 p.m.
On Tuesday, I am going to watch a film on TV at 8.15.
On Wednesday, I am going to learn for a German test with Tom.
On Thursday, I am going to help Kate with her maths homework.
On Friday, I am going to buy a birthday present for Sarah; then I am going to ring her up.
On Saturday, I am going to go to Sarah's birthday party.
On Sunday, I am going to ring up Tom and go for a walk with him ...

Training 3

On Monday, I am going to play football.
On Tuesday, I am going to ...
On Wednesday, ...
etc.

Training 4

1. Today I am ill.
2. Today I needn't get up.
3. Today I can stay in bed.
4. Today I needn't go to school.
5. Today I needn't do any homework.
6. Today I have got no German.
7. Today I have got a temperature.
8. Today is a beautiful day.

Training 5

Sarah:
Brr ... Pudding again. I really don't like pudding.

Christine:
Ugh ... Sausages. I had them yesterday. I can't eat sausages every day.

Joe:
... I had an egg this morning. I don't want another egg now.

Tom:
I like chocolate pudding. If you don't want your chocolate pudding, you can give it to me.

Sandra to Kevin:
... I could eat chips from morning to night.

Kevin:
... I think I'll have it. Do you take fruit salad, too, Sandra?

Training 6

1. English pupils already go to school when they are five.
2. Most British pupils go to a comprehensive school when they are eleven.
3. They can leave school when they are 16.
4. In many schools they must wear school uniform.

5. The school colours in Tom's school are blue and grey.
6. The pupils' parents can buy the school uniforms in special shops.
7. In most English schools lessons begin later than in Germany.
8. Most English pupils also have lessons in the afternoon.
9. There are lessons in the afternoon, so many English schools have school cafeterias.
10. Pupils can have lunch at the school cafetiera during break.
11. In many English schools pupils learn to cook.

Training 7

Mögliche Fragen:
– What subjects do you have on Monday?
– What do you have in the first lesson?
– What do you do in the break?
– When and where do you see Jenny?

Mögliche Antworten:
– On Monday, I have got maths, biology, geography, English and German.
– In the first two lessons I have got maths. In the third and fourth lesson I have got biology. In the afternoon I first have geography, then English. My last lesson on Monday is German.
– In the break I talk to Jenny/I play with Mike …
– I see Jenny every morning and every afternoon. She is in my class!
– Usually I have lunch at home, but sometimes I have lunch in the school cafeteria, too.
– I usually do my homework when I come home from school.
– I usually do it in my room.

Training 8

There are pupils
– who usually forget their homework.
– who have never forgotten their homework.
– who often do their homework at school.
– who have never copied it from their neighbours.
– who never know what they must do.
– who never write down what they must do.
– who always forget their homework at home.
– who usually do it on the way to school.
– who sometimes leave their exercise book at home.
– who sometimes forget it on the bus.

Training 9

Mögliche Antworten:

1. I usually do my homework./Yes, I do.
2. I usually/always do it in the afternoon/in the evening/in the morning.
3. I usually do it at home/on the bus/at school.
4. I don't usually forget it./No, I don't.
5. I sometimes forget it when I have got no time/when I don't think of it.
6. I never copy it from my neighbour./No, never. I only sometimes copy it from him.
7. No, I'm not. I usually play with my neighbour or talk to him.
8. No, they don't. They don't often help me/Yes, they do. They often help me.
9. He often helps me in ...
10. Yes, he has/No, he hasn't. He has never helped me.